THE CHURCH EARNESTLY DESIRES THAT
ALL THE FAITHFUL BE LED TO THAT
FULL, CONSCIOUS, AND ACTIVE
PARTICIPATION IN LITURGICAL
CELEBRATIONS CALLED FOR BY THE
VERY NATURE OF THE LITURGY◻
SUCH PARTICIPATION BY THE
CHRISTIAN PEOPLE AS ›A CHOSEN RACE,
A ROYAL PRIESTHOOD, A HOLY
NATION, GOD'S OWN PEOPLE‹ (1 PETER 2:9
SEE 2:4-5)
IS THEIR RIGHT AND DUTY BY REASON
OF THEIR BAPTISM◻ IN THE REFORM
AND PROMOTION OF THE LITURGY,
THIS FULL AND ACTIVE PARTICIPATION
BY ALL THE PEOPLE IS THE AIM TO BE
CONSIDERED BEFORE ALL ELSE◻
FOR IT IS THE PRIMARY AND
INDISPENSABLE SOURCE FROM
WHICH THE FAITHFUL ARE TO DERIVE
THE TRUE CHRISTIAN SPIRIT◻

THE CHURCH EARNESTLY DESIRES THAT ALL THE FAITHFUL BE LED TO THAT FULLY CONSCIOUS AND ACTIVE PARTICIPATION IN LITURGICAL CELEBRATIONS CALLED FOR BY THE VERY NATURE OF THE LITURGY. SUCH PARTICIPATION BY THE CHRISTIAN PEOPLE AS A CHOSEN RACE, A ROYAL PRIESTHOOD, A HOLY NATION, GOD'S OWN PEOPLE (1 PETER 2:9 SEE 2:4-5) IS THEIR RIGHT AND DUTY BY REASON OF THEIR BAPTISM. IN THE REFORM AND PROMOTION OF THE LITURGY, THIS FULL AND ACTIVE PARTICIPATION BY ALL THE PEOPLE IS THE AIM TO BE CONSIDERED BEFORE ALL ELSE. FOR IT IS THE PRIMARY AND INDISPENSABLE SOURCE FROM WHICH THE FAITHFUL ARE TO DERIVE THE TRUE CHRISTIAN SPIRIT.

A Sourcebook about Liturgy

Also in the Sourcebook Series:

A Lent Sourcebook: The Forty Days (two volumes)

A Triduum Sourcebook

An Easter Soucebook: The Fifty Days

An Advent Sourcebook

A Christmas Sourcebook

A Baptism Sourcebook

A Marriage Sourcebook

A Sourcebook about Christian Death

A Sourcebook about Liturgy

Edited by
Gabe Huck

Art by
Vivian Carter

LTP
Liturgy Training Publications

Acknowledgments

First our thanks to those who wrote and spoke the words on these pages, then to those who shared these texts with the editor and the readers. All the people who submitted texts are named in the introduction.

We are grateful to the many publishers and authors who have given permission to include their work. Every effort has been made to determine the ownership of all texts and to make proper arrangements for their use. We will gladly correct in future editions any oversight or error that is brought to our attention.

Acknowledgment of all sources will be found in the endnotes.

Editorial assistance: Jennifer McGeary and Lorraine Schmidt
Production: Judy Sweetwood
Typesetter: Jim Mellody-Pizzato
Series designer: Michael Tapia

Copyright © 1994, Archdiocese of Chicago: Liturgy Training Publications, 1800 North Hermitage Avenue, Chicago IL 60622-1101; 1-800-933-1800, FAX 1-800-933-7094. All rights reserved.

LITSB
$12.95

Printed in the United States of America

Library of Congress Cataloging-in-Publication Data

A sourcebook about liturgy / edited by Gabe Huck.
     p.   cm.
    Includes bibliographical references.
    ISBN 1-56854-029-9 : $12.95
     1. Liturgics—Quotations, maxims, etc. I. Huck, Gabe.
II. Title: Sourcebook about liturgy.
BV178.S64 1994
264—dc20
                                      94-3514
                                      CIP

Contents

Introduction

The preceding two pages should not be called a table of contents. They don't give the reader the solid information one should expect. At best they look like the titles in a poetry anthology: useful only if you know what poem you're looking for.

But they do make an interesting list: "This Kiss Blends Souls"; "Smelling of the Good Work"; "Sing the World to Sleep." What are we doing here?

It was not obvious how to arrange these texts. Alphabetical by author as in some quotation collections would have been one way. Anything else risks editorializing. So let the reader beware! Your arrangement might have been far different. Every phrase in the contents list is taken from a quote, and those are the quotes that signal subtle or obvious changes of direction as you meander through this book (watch for the art in the margin and the changes in the running heads on each page). Second guessing the editor by mentally rearranging these texts would be an excellent thing to do. Another would be adding marginal notes for quotes that should have been included and were not.

Of what possible use is such a book? All the other books in this series have their times and occasions. This one does not. It is perhaps the weft to the warp of the others. But, like its subject matter, is has no obvious practicality.

The question behind this collection of texts is: What texts about the liturgy do you love? I sent that question to about 50 people: musicians, writers, artists, scholars, pastors and other practitioners. I asked them to think beyond the narrow confines and to remember fiction and poetry and all sorts of writing. More than half responded with far more texts than made the final cut. As would be expected, some of the same texts showed up from multiple senders.

These are the people to be thanked: John Baldovin, SJ; Eleanor Bernstein, CSJ; Agnes Cunningham, SSCM; Linda Ekstrom; Steve Erspamer, SM; Edward Foley, CAPUCHIN; Mark R. Francis, CSV; Virgil C. Funk (with assistance from Nancy Chvatal,

Gordon Truitt, Lisa Tarker); Genevieve Glen, OSB; Charles W. Gusmer, STD; Joan Halmo; Kathleen Hughes, RSCJ; Rosa Maria Icaza; Dennis W. Krouse; Gordon Lathrop; Ron Lewinski; Mary McGann, RSCJ; John Melloh, SM; Nathan Mitchell; Melissa Musick Nussbaum; David Philippart; Gail Ramshaw; Adam Redjinski; Mary Frances Reza; G. Thomas Ryan; James M. Schellman; Thomas G. Simons; Virginia Sloyan; Dennis C. Smolarski, SJ; Janet R. Walton; Louis Weil.

This book, then, is simply the texts that have brought insight, delight and challenge to the people above in their love of liturgy. These are not necessarily the "important" texts in any scholarly sense. They are the texts that showed the way, the texts these people fell in love with, the ones they look at again and again and say Amen. It is no surprise then that we'll find a few quarrels among the texts on these pages.

Is there good balance here? It is probably too full of the last several generations. The number of women is not what it will be next time one of these books is done, nor is the proportion of texts from outside the European tradition. Quite probably there are some very recently written texts here that won't survive. The texts that come from surprising places (i.e., not books about liturgy and church) are numerous but perhaps not yet the proportion they could be. For all these reasons, let the reader beware!

Throughout the book, when noninclusive language could be changed without calling attention to the change, this has been done.

These sourcebooks are for reading a little at a time, pencil in hand or at least always ready to fold over the corner of a page for a return visit. In some cases, with the help of the endnotes, the reader will want to find the place these words came from and read more and more. In other cases, an appropriate text might be clipped to find its way to a bathroom mirror or a sacristy door. The hope is that a few of them will, for each person who takes up this book, unfold and so make even more filled with mystery the rituals we have been given and are giving.

Gabe Huck

I cannot achieve contemplation, as some can; and so, having to face and forgive my own failures, I have learned from them both the necessity and wonder of ritual. For ritual allows those who cannot will themselves out of the secular to perform the spiritual, as dancing allows the tongue-tied a ceremony of love.

Andre Dubus

THERE is a modest and essential place in every liturgical celebration for human rhetoric, but it is a modest place, subordinate to the proclamation of the word of God in scripture, subordinate to the symbolic action of the whole assembly. Implied in all this is the conviction that what is most important about public worship is that we gather the sisters and brothers together for a festival, a special occasion, a celebration of the reign of God (not yet terribly evident in daily life nor in the institutions of society), that helps all of us feel so good about ourselves, so important, so dignified, so precious, so free, so much at one . . . not as escape, not merely in distinction to daily routine, but in judgment, in the Lord's judgment on those ways and institutions. A celebration of the reign of God that goes way beyond the tight, drab, rationalistic, verbose, pedagogical exercises we sometimes try to make of it—all those dreadful "themes" that we love—into a large, broad, fully human landscape, where Jesus is truly the firstborn of a new humanity, and where our other liturgical tools (festival excess and colors and tastes and textures and odors and forms and touches) penetrate the Babel of our words and points and arguments to heal the human spirit and to raise it up in the covenant community's vision of new possibilities. Good liturgical celebration, like a parable, takes us by the hair of our heads, lifts us momentarily out of the cesspool of injustice we call home, puts us in the promised and challenging reign of God, where we are treated like we have never been treated anywhere else.

Robert W. Hovda

CREATION often
needs two hearts
one to root
and one to flower
One to sustain
in time of drouth
and hold fast
against winds of pain
the fragile bloom
that in the glory
of its hour
affirms a heart
unsung, unseen.

Marilou Awiakta

IT is either short-sighted or vainglorious to assume that self-expression as such is the supreme goal of prayer. The supreme goal of prayer is to express God, to discover the self in relation to God.

Abraham Joshua
Heschel

TO be a person of prayer, some might say, it is not necessary to consecrate certain times to prayer; we can find God in everything. This is perfectly true. Nevertheless, we begin to be able to find God in everything when we have begun by finding God above and beyond everything. It is practically impossible to lead a life of union with God so long as there has not been that minimum of formal prayer which allows us to acquire spiritual liberty by accustoming us to disengagement from the chains of our environment.

Jean Daniélou

I undressed, dove into the sea, and swam. I felt the sacrament of baptism in all its deathless simplicity on that day, understood why so many religions consider water and the bath, in other words baptism, the indispensable, presupposed condition of initiation before a convert begins new life. The water's coolness penetrates to the marrow of the bones, to the very pith; it finds the soul, and this, seeing the water, beats its wings happily like a young sea gull, washes itself, rejoices, and is refreshed. The simple everyday water is transubstantiated; it becomes the water of eternal life and renews the person. When the convert emerges from the water, the world seem changed. The world has not changed, it is always wonderful and horrible, iniquitous and filled with beauty. But now, after baptism, the eyes that see the world have changed.

Nikos Kazantzakis

DURING a feast we feel ourselves transferred to a different world. A skeptic will call this an illusion because the world goes on just the same and no ladders appear to bear us to the sky. Is it really an illusion? At a feast we live in an inward world of longings and fantasies, in plans one has in mind and wants to carry out. Reality is lit up by this ideal as the sun lights up a landscape. Without the sun, things remain what they are: In its light they shine with what they want and could be. The feast, born of the spirit, transforms reality; and life infused from within, reveals treasures, harmonies and dynamisms that cannot be appreciated by the rough contact of hands. Being poetry, it guesses what is hidden beneath an opaque rind. Those who feast live in a new world, which is their own seen through prophetic eyes; they go out to meet the good world created by God and for them it is brother and sister not enemy.

Juan Mateos

WHEN the liturgy is genuinely lived, when rising up as the divine hymn of silence it enters the gates of the recollected soul, its power of reconciliation cannot be told.

Everything bows peacefully to the redemptive demands of crucified love. Gestures turn inwards, words become silent, chants listen, colors set forth the soul's seasons, incense

Maurice Zundel

bears her prayer aloft, the whole of matter offers the depths of its being to be the tabernacle of the Spirit. Creation is seen from within transparent in the living unity of love.

THE Ascension is a festival of the future of the world. The flesh is redeemed and glorified, for the Lord has risen for ever. We Christians are, therefore, the most sublime of materialists. We neither can nor should conceive of any ultimate fullness of the spirit and of reality without thinking too of matter enduring as well in a state of final perfection. It is true that we cannot picture to ourselves in the concrete how matter would have to appear in this state of final endurance and glorification for all eternity. But we have so to love our own physicality and the worldly environment appropriate to it that we cannot reconcile ourselves to conceiving of ourselves as existing to all eternity otherwise than with the material side of our natures enduring too in a state of final perfection. And—one shudders at the "blasphemy" which such an idea must represent for the Greek mentality—we could not conceive of the divine Logos either in the eternal perfection which belongs to it for ever otherwise than as existing for ever in the state of material incarnation which it has assumed. As materialists we are more crassly materialist than those who call themselves so. For among these it would still be possible to imagine that matter as a whole and in its entirety could, so to say, be raised at one blow onto a new plane and undergo a radical qualitative change such that, for purposes of definition, it could no longer be called matter because this future state would be so utterly different from the former one in which it originated. We can entertain no such theory. We recognise and believe that this matter will last for ever, and be glorified for ever. It must be glorified. It must undergo a transformation the depths of which we can only sense with fear and trembling in that process which we experience as our death. But it remains. It continues to perform its function for ever. It celebrates a festival that lasts for ever. . . . The Ascension is the festival of the true future of the world. The festival we are celebrating is an eschatological one. In this celebration we anticipate the festival of the universal and glorious transfiguration of the world which has already commenced, and which, since the ascension, has been ripening and developing towards the point where it will become manifest.   Karl Rahner

B UT when Jesus took bread and wine or a few fish and blessed God for them and shared them with his disciples, creation found its purpose once again. When the wood of the cross, itself the innocent victim and unchoosing collaborator in inhumanity, became the means of expressing a hitherto undreamed of relationship between God and God's people, the wood itself was redeemed. In each instance the true order of things was restored and justice reigned insofar as created things could now once again speak of God, the "lover of the human race." At the same time, and inseparably, they spoke of the right relationship that should exist between human beings. When Jesus took the bread, said the blessing, broke the bread and shared it, he demonstrated, unforgettably, the proper use of all material things. The early Christians realized this: They "eucharistized" their lives by blessing God in all things and by making their possessions available to one another. And when Jesus took the cup and gave thanks to God and passed it among his disciples, he rediscovered for the human race the joy of not claiming anything for one's own—not even life itself.   Mark Searle

T O name a thing, in other words, is to bless God for it and in it. And in the Bible to bless God is not a "religious" or a "cultic" act, but the very *way of life*. God blessed the world, blessed the human beings, blessed the seventh day (that is, time), and this means that God filled all that exists with love and goodness, made all this "very good." So the only *natural* (and not "supernatural") reaction of ourselves, to whom God gave this blessed and sanctified world, is to bless God in return, to thank God, to *see* the world as God sees it and—in this act of gratitude and adoration—to know, name and possess the world. All our rational, spiritual and other qualities distinguishing us from other creatures, have their focus and ultimate fulfillment in this capacity to bless God, to know, so to speak, the meaning of the thirst and hunger that constitutes God's life. *"Homo sapiens," "homo faber"* . . . yes, but, first of all, *"homo adorans."* We stand in the center of the world and unify it in our act of blessing God, of both receiving the world from God and offering it to God—and by filling the world with this eucharist, we transform our lives, the ones that we receive from the world, into life in God, into communion with God. The world was created as the "matter," the material of one all-embracing eucharist, and we were created as priest of this cosmic statement.

Alexander Schmemann

To the total offer that is made me, I can only answer by a total acceptance. I shall therefore react to the eucharistic contact with *the entire effort of my life*—of my life of today and of my life of tomorrow, of my personal life and of my life as linked to all other lives. Periodically, the sacred species may perhaps fade away in me. But each time they will leave me a little more deeply engulfed in the layers of your omnipresence: Living and dying, I shall never at any moment cease to move forward in you. Thus the precept implicit in your church, that we must communicate everywhere and always, is justified with extraordinary force and precision. The eucharist must invade my life. My life must become, as a result of the sacrament, an unlimited and endless contact with you—that life which seemed, a few moments ago, like a baptism with you in the waters of the world, now reveals itself to me as communion with you through the world. It is the sacrament of life. *The sacrament of my life*—of my life received, of my life lived, of my life surrendered.

Pierre Teilhard de Chardin

...hip implies "to do," to work and collaborate in the construction of the earthly city, being at the same time very conscious that this city has a dimension which transcends what is visible at first sight, that the city of God is not a second city, but the real world of which the appearance is precisely this, our visible world. To build up, to discover, to create, to accelerate the human process or the coming of the kingdom—or whatever expression we may here choose—this too is the function of worship today. . . . The classical conception of sacrifice in practically all religions is, in fact, intimately connected with the aspect of worship. The ultimate function of sacrifice is to let the whole world reach its destination, to re-create the world, to let time, the *saeculum,* continue.

Raimondo Panikkar

THE Christian hope of the future is that this, the true meaning and message of the incarnation, will come to be more deeply understood, and the demand on our worshiping love and total self-offering will receive a more complete response—a response stretching upward in awestruck contemplation to share that adoring vision of the Principle which is "the inheritance of the saints in light," and downwards and outwards in loving action, to embrace and so transform the whole world. When this happens, Christian sacramental worship will at last disclose its full meaning, and enter into its full heritage. For it will be recognized as the ritual sign of our deepest relation with Reality, and so of the mysterious splendour of our situation and our call: our successive life freely offered in oblation, and the abiding life of God in Christ received, not for our own sakes, but in order to achieve that transfiguration of the whole created universe, that shining forth of the splendour of the Holy, in which the aim of worship shall be fulfilled.

Evelyn Underhill

L OOK, the trees
are turning
their own bodies
into pillars

of light,
are giving off the rich
fragrance of cinnamon
and fulfillment,

the long tapers
of cattails
are bursting and floating away over
the blue shoulders

of the ponds,
and every pond,
no matter what its
name is, is

nameless now.
Every year
everything
I have ever learned

in my lifetime
leads back to this: the fires
and the black river of loss
whose other side

is salvation,
whose meaning
none of us will ever know.
To live in this world

you must be able
to do three things:
to love what is mortal;
to hold it

against your bones knowing
your own life depends on it;
and, when the time comes to let it go,
to let it go.

Mary Oliver

City, when we see you coming down,
   Coming down from God
To be the new world's crown:
How shall they sing, the fresh, unsalted seas
Hearing your harmonies!

For there is no more death,
No need to cure those waters, now, with any brine;
Their shores give them no dead,
Rivers no blood, no rot to stain them.

Because the cruel algebra of war
Is now no more.
And the steel circle of time, inexorable,
Bites like a padlock shut, forever,
In the smoke of the last bomb:
And in that trap the murderers
     and sorcerers and crooked leaders
Go rolling home to hell.
And history is done.

Shine with your lamb-light, shine upon the world:
You are the new creation's sun.
And standing on their twelve foundations,
Lo, the twelve gates that are One Christ are wide
     as canticles:

And Oh! Begin to hear the thunder of the songs
     within the crystal Towers,
While all the saints rise from their earth with feet like light
And fly to tread the quick-gold of those streets,

Oh, City, when we see you sailing down,
Sailing down from God,
Dressed in the glory of the Trinity, and angel-crowned
Thomas Merton   In nine white diadems of liturgy.

YOU enter into the room of a king
     or a great lord,
          or, I believe, they call it
               the treasure chamber,
where there are countless kinds
     of glass and earthen vessels
     and other things so arranged
          that upon entering
     the soul sees almost all these objects.

The soul, while it is made one with God,
     is placed in this room of treasures
          that we must have interiorly.
After it returns to itself
     the soul is left with the representation
          of the grandeurs it saw,
     but it cannot describe any of them.

In a rapture, God carries off
     the entire soul, and, as to someone who is
          God's spouse,
     begins showing it some little part
     of the kingdom it has gained
Teresa of Avila   by being espoused to God.

FOR baptism signifies that the old one and the sinful birth of flesh and blood are to be wholly drowned by the grace of God. We should therefore do justice to its meaning and make baptism a true and complete sign of the thing it signifies.

Martin Luther
Sixteenth century

THERE is the story of the Russian envoys who after a visit to Constantinople were so impressed with the liturgy there that they returned to Russia proclaiming they had been in heaven. The story may or may not be historically true, but it does express a great truth nevertheless. Authentic Christian worship must always convey something of the impression— a reflection of the glory of the *Christos Kyrios*—the majesty of the King of Glory. For it is the glorified Christ who stands in the midst of his disciples and brings them his message of heavenly peace. His presence in our worship means that the world to come, the *vitam venturi saeculi,* breaks in upon this world, and heaven comes down to earth. During the days of our life here on earth we already partake of the kingdom that is to come. We enter into the new order of things inaugurated by Christ on the day of his ascension. The divine service of the church is at the same time the worship of pilgrims and travellers on this earth and the worship of citizens of the heavenly city who have already come to the end of their pilgrimage. For "we have not here a lasting city" and "our manner of living is in the heavens."

William J. O'Shea

JUDGE, every year on the Thursday before Good Friday we have in the Holy Church of Zion the service of the Washing of the Feet. Many people from other churches come to see it, and they are satisfied. This year the minister, that is myself, is going to wash the feet of Mrs. Hannah Mofokeng, who is the oldest woman in Bochabela. And my daughter is going to wash the feet of Esther Moloi, who is a crippled child. And I am asking Judge Olivier to wash the feet of Martha Fortuin.

—Martha?

—Yes, judge.

—She has washed the feet of all my children. Why should I hesitate to wash her feet?

Mr. Buti's face was filled with joy. He stood up and opened wide his arms.

—Do you understand, judge, I want our people to see that their love is not rejected. Do you see that?

—Yes, I can see that.

—It will be simple, judge. I shall call out the name of Martha Fortuin, and she will come up and take a seat at the front of the altar. Then I shall call out the name of Jan Christiaan Olivier—you will not mind, judge, if I do not call you a judge?

—No.

—Then you come up to the altar, and I shall give you a towel to put round yourself, and then a basin of water. I shall take off her shoes, and you will wash her feet and dry them, and go back to your seat. Then I shall put on her shoes, and she will go back to her seat.

—Does she know that I am to wash her feet?

—She knows that her feet are to be washed, but she does not know who is going to wash them.

—Will she be embarrassed?

—I do not think so, judge. She is a holy woman. She knows the meaning of it. After all, the disciples' feet were washed by the Lord, and no one was embarrassed but Peter, and he was rebuked for it.

—There's one thing more, Mr. Buti.

—Yes, judge.

—She does not know. Then who does know?

—Only myself and my elders. And of course you, judge.

—Well, that is proper. You see, Mr. Buti, a judge can do this kind of thing privately. He is as free to do it as anyone else. But a judge must not parade himself—you understand?— he must not . . .

—I understand, judge. Judge, you have made my heart glad. For me, and for many of my people, this will be a work of healing. I hope for our young people too. You know, judge, some of them think that white people do not know how to love, so why should they love them? I told them that Jesus said we must love our enemies, and one bright boy said to me that Jesus did not live in Bochabela. . . .

Then Mr. Buti gave the towel to the judge, and the judge, as the word says, girded himself with it, and took the dish of water and knelt at the feet of Martha Fortuin. He took her right foot in his hands and washed it and dried it with the towel. Then he took her other foot in his hands and washed it and dried it with the towel. Then he took both her feet in his hands with gentleness, for they were no doubt tired with much serving, and he kissed them both.   Alan Paton

A meal celebrated in prospect of the coming reign of God must give rise to a new social vision grounded in the promise of the kingdom. Such a vision challenges the status quo in society and the prevailing set of economic and social relationships. Sharing in a community meal anticipates a just sharing of all the gifts of creation in justice and love. It must give rise to a new set of relationships in society that reflect that vision. The community that celebrates the eucharist in prospect of the kingdom must ask itself whether its tablesharing in the eucharist is reflected in a just sharing of the gifts of the earth or whether some are deprived of the means of life because others hoard the world's goods for their own advantage. Eucharistic participation must lead first of all to a new social vision, then to a critique of our existing society in the light of that vision, and finally to advocacy for the poor and disadvantaged members of society and to social change. The community gathered around the table of the Lord must be prepared to have its entire common life in the world placed under both judgment and grace.   William R. Crockett

THE liturgical worship of any local community discloses a vision of what it means to live as a Christian. It does this through the symbols, language, actions, interactions, relationships that constitute the ritual performance. Within this horizon certain beliefs, memories, values and hopes will be made available from the Christian tapestry of meaning for the personal appropriation of members of the assembly. Others will be kept out. Those that are admitted may be enhanced, impoverished, modified in some way to fit the situation. Sometimes they may even be distorted. In the process of mediating a public corporate horizon for a community, liturgy sets limits for the Christian imagination and thus acts as a censor in the construction of Christian identity.

Margaret Mary
Kelleher

N OW we urge you to praise God. That is what we are all telling each other when we say *Alleluia.* You say to your neighbor, "Praise the Lord!" and your neighbor says the same to you. We are all urging one another to praise the Lord, and all thereby doing what each of us urges the other to do. But see that your praise comes from your whole being; in other words, see that you praise God not with your lips and voices alone, but with your minds, your lives and all your actions.

We are praising God now, assembled as we are here in church; but when we go our various ways again, it seems as if we cease to praise God. But provided we do not cease to live a good life, we shall always be praising God. You cease to praise God only when you swerve from justice and from what is pleasing to God. If you never turn aside from the good life, your tongue may be silent but your actions will cry aloud, and God will perceive your intentions; for as our ears hear each other's voices, so do God's ears hear our thoughts.

Augustine
Fifth century

W HEN the liturgy is given a political theme without allowing the celebration to show its existential dynamics, the inadequacy is increased rather than reduced. The faithful are more indoctrinated than converted, and more convicted of guilt than liberated.

Joseph Gelineau

HOW, then, can we continually receive the eucharistic Christ and leave untouched or unchanged any bitter or hardened prejudice against any member of any race of people? We tell ourselves that we mean no harm to anyone. Yet at the same time, we repeat the cheap racial joke, we make the ill-advised remark, we indulge in self-righteous anger in the home—all these plant the seed of a whole new generation of prejudice in our children. It seems so unimportant, so trivial. But multiply it by thousands and it becomes a cancer of sinful attitudes which sickens and weakens the body of the church. Small wonder that men ask how can it be the *same* Christ that we love. . . .

Liturgy understood as *the worship* of the church and social action understood as *the work* of the church are part, one of the other. Liturgy which does not move its participants to social action is mere ceremonialism; social action which does not find its source in the liturgy is mere humanitarianism.   Richard Cushing

THE success of liturgical restoration is closely interwoven with social and political action. We can't reasonably pray for peace unless we are working for peace. We can't eat the food of salvation in good conscience so long as anyone goes unfed or unhoused. For the length of time that anyone can't eat and sleep where others can eat and sleep, our celebrations of the mystery of Christ will ring hollow.

They will be signs of community to which there corresponds no genuine reality of community.   Gerard S. Sloyan

THE commitment I envision must be in our Catholic bones: the need to assemble each Sunday, to make common prayer in song, to hear the scriptures and reflect on them, to intercede for all the world, to gather at the holy table and give God thanks and praise over the bread and wine which are for us the body and blood of our Lord Jesus Christ, and finally to go from that room to our separate worlds—but now carrying the tune we have heard, murmuring the words we have made ours, nourished by the sacred banquet, ready in so many ways to make all God's creation and all the work of human hands into the kingdom we have glimpsed in the liturgy. . . .

At this table we put aside every worldly separation based on culture, class, or other differences. Baptized, we no longer admit to distinctions based on age or sex or race or wealth. This communion is why all prejudice, all racism, all sexism, all deference to wealth and power must be banished from our parishes, our homes, and our lives. This communion is why we will not call enemies those who are human beings like ourselves. This communion is why we will not commit the world's resources to an escalating arms race while the poor die. We cannot. Not when we have feasted here on the "body broken" and "blood poured out" for the life of the world.

Joseph Bernardin

I simply can't talk about the creation of recognizable communities of faith, viable churches, without a primary witness to what I consider almost the sole glory of the Catholic churches, which have borne the heavy burden and paid the sometimes almost intolerable price of unity, of keeping a unity with the other churches around the see of Rome. If we have anything to bring to the absolutely necessary general unity of the Christian churches, it is this passion for communion, this fanatical insistence on concrete relations between human local churches, on the *fermentum,* on the local church as essentially outward-looking, stretching out its arms (especially in social action, in sacrament, in ministry) not only to the other churches but, as a sign of unity, to the whole human family. If the church does not witness to this earthy, common, dirty, stinky, glorious human relationship between the churches, between the communities of faith, it may witness to a thousand things, but it misses the point, *the* point of poignant priority.

Robert W. Hovda

VICTOR, who presided at Rome, immediately tried to cut off from the common unity the dioceses of all Asia, together with the adjacent churches, on the ground of heterodoxy, and he indited letters announcing that all the Christians there were absolutely excommunicated. But by no means all were pleased by this, so they issued counter-requests to him to consider the cause of peace and unity and love towards his neighbours. Their words are extant, sharply rebuking Victor. Among them too Irenaeus, writing in the name of the Christians whose leader he was in Gaul, though he recommends that the mystery of the Lord's resurrection be observed only on the Lord's day, yet nevertheless exhorts Victor suitably and at length not to excommunicate whole churches of God for following a tradition of ancient custom, and continues as follows: "For the controversy is not only about the day, but also about the actual character of the fast; for some think that they ought to fast one day, others two, others even more, some count their day as forty hours, day and night. And such variation of observance did not begin in our own time, but much earlier, in the day of our predecessors who, it would appear, disregarding strictness maintained a practice which is simple and yet allows for personal reference, establishing it for the future, and none the less all these lived in peace, and we also live in peace with one another and the disagreement in the fast confirms our agreement in the faith."

He adds to this a narrative which I may suitably quote, running as follows: "Among those too were the presbyters before Soter, who presided over the church of which you are now the leader, I mean Anicetus and Pius and Telesphorus and Xystus. They did not themselves observe it, nor did they enjoin it on those who followed them, and though they did not keep it they were none the less at peace with those from the dioceses in which it was observed when they came to them, although to observe it was more objectionable to those who did not do so. And no one was ever rejected for this reason, but the presbyters before you who did not observe it sent the eucharist to those from other dioceses who did; and when the blessed Polycarp was staying in Rome in the time of Anicetus, though they disagreed a little about some other things as well, they immediately made peace, having no wish for strife between them on this matter. For neither was Anicetus able to persuade Polycarp not to observe it, inasmuch as he had always done so in company with John the disciple of our Lord and the other apostles with whom he had associated; nor did Polycarp persuade Anicetus to observe it, for he said that he ought to keep the custom of those who were presbyters before him. And under these circumstances they communicated with each other, and in the church Anicetus yielded the celebration of the eucharist to Polycarp, obviously out of respect, and they parted from each other in peace, for the peace of the whole church was kept both by those who observed and by those who did not."

Eusebius
Fourth century

As I was nearing the end of the evangelization of the first six Masai communities, I began looking towards baptism. So I went to the old man Ndangoya's community to prepare them for the final step.

I told them I had finished the imparting of the Christian message inasmuch as I could. I had taught them everything I knew about Christianity. Now it was up to them. They could reject it or accept it. I could do no more. If they did accept it, of course, it required public baptism. So I would go away for a week or so and give them the opportunity to make their judgment on the gospel of Jesus Christ. If they did accept it, then there would be baptism. However, baptism wasn't automatic. Over the course of the year it had taken me to instruct them, I had gotten to know them very well indeed.

So I stood in front of the assembled community and began: "This old man sitting here has missed too many of our instruction meetings. He was always out herding cattle. He will not be baptized with the rest. These two on this side will be baptized because they always attended, and understood very well what we talked about. So did this young mother. She will be baptized. But that man there has obviously not understood the instructions. And that lady there has scarcely believed the gospel message. They cannot be baptized. And this warrior has not shown enough effort. . . ."

The old man, Ndangoya, stopped me politely but firmly, "Padri, why are you trying to break us up and separate us? During this whole year that you have been teaching us, we have talked about these things when you were not here, at night around the fire. Yes, there have been lazy ones in this community. But they have been helped by those with much energy. There are stupid ones in the community, but they have been helped by those who are intelligent. Yes, there are ones with little faith in this village, but they have been helped by those with much faith. Would you turn out and drive off the lazy ones and the one with little faith and the stupid ones? From the first day I have spoken for these people. And I speak for them now. Now, on this day one year later, I can declare for them and for all this community, that we have reached the step in our lives where we can say, 'We believe.'"

Vincent Donovan

THE primary and exclusive aim of the liturgy is not the expression of the individual's reverence and worship for God. It is not even concerned with the awakening, formation and sanctification of the individual soul as such. Nor does the onus of liturgical action and prayer rest with the individual. It does not even rest with the collective groups, composed of numerous individuals, who periodically achieve a limited and intermittent unity in their capacity as the congregation of a church. The liturgical entity consists rather of the united body of the faithful as such—the church—a body which infinitely outnumbers the mere congregation.

Romano Guardini

TRUE worship is that continual occasioning through time of the divine-human dialogue, the ongoing prayer of Christ in his people animated by the Holy Spirit. The central mystery of Christian life and worship is found here: Christ prays in the world for the world, in and through our prayers in his name. And in the symbols that convey the reality and power of death and resurrection, our worship draws us into the very life of God—now and in the Kingdom come.

Don E. Saliers

NEITHER the vigil nor a funeral (nor for that matter a wedding or an ordination) is liturgy "for" someone. These are celebrations of the church, by the church, and for the church under the criteria of the gospel.

Marilou Awiakta

SACRAMENT, that is, liturgy, is the existential, common expression of God's self-giving in Christ. It is a theophany, a breaking into the ordinary of an extraordinary manifestation of Christ as being-in-his-Body, the church. It makes the inner experience of the life of faith transparent, visible. Here too, then, faith is required. Once again, this is not to make the presence subjective, to make God's saving action a hostage to our faith. Christ's presence does not depend on the individual's faith nor is it caused by faith independently of Christ's Spirit. But it is dependent on the faith of the church, for without that apostolic *Antwort* it would never have come into being. And it depends on individual faith to be personalized in each of us, for only faith draws back the veil. As Origen said in his *Commentary on Romans* 4:2, "We see one thing but understand another. We see a man [that is, Jesus], but believe in God." This is the basis of Origen's theology of the sacraments: We see a water bath but believe in another, greater cleansing; we see bread and wine but believe in a higher food, the body and blood of Christ. In so doing we believe in Jesus' "for-us," which is the basis of our "for-one-another" in him, as our only possible *Antwort* to him, which is, in turn, the basis of all Christian life.

Robert Taft

I T is not safe to pray alone. Tradition insists that we pray with, and as a part of, the community; that public worship is preferable to private worship. Here we are faced with an aspect of the *polarity of prayer*. There is a permanent union between individual worship and community worship, each of which depends for its existence upon the other. To ignore their *spiritual symbiosis* will prove fatal to both.

How can we forget that our ability to pray we owe to the community and to tradition? We have learned how to pray by listening to the voice of prayer, by having been a part of a community standing before God.

Those who cherish genuine prayer, yet feel driven away from the houses of worship because of the sterility of public worship today, seem to believe that private prayer is the only way. Yet, the truth is that private prayer will not survive unless it is inspired by public prayer.

Abraham Joshua Heschel

W HAT do people do when they assemble to worship? They seek out each other's company to acknowledge the Love that surrounds them, attracts them, impels them. If they live their lives regularly in the presence of the Holy and gather on Sunday to do the same in common, coming together in this way makes eminently good sense. If they do not live their lives in God's presence, regular assembly *may* lead to a posture of awe, but this is by no means assured.

Gerard S. Sloyan

T HEY devoted themselves to the teaching of the apostles and to the communal life, to the breaking of the bread and to the prayers. Awe came upon everyone, and many wonders and signs were done through the apostles. All who believed were together and had all things in common; they would sell their property and possessions and divide them among all according to each one's need. Every day they devoted themselves to meeting together in the temple area and to breaking bread in their homes. They ate their meals with exultation and sincerity of heart, praising God and enjoying favor with all the people. And every day the Lord added to their number those who were being saved.

Acts 2:42–47

THE morning after my bar mitzva, I returned with Pop to the synagogue. What a contrast! Gloomy, silent, all but empty; down front, Morris Elfenbein and a few old men putting on prayer shawls and phylacteries, *t'filin.* I had my new phylacteries, and Mar Weil had taught me how to tie them on. Before my bar mitzva I had been ineligible to utter God's name in the blessings; I now recited them as I fastened on the black leather boxes, with Pop's eyes shining at me. That was good, but otherwise, what a letdown! Without me they'd actually have lacked the minyan, the quorum of ten men.

We American Jews have strange ways. Most of us tend to take the bar-mitzva blowout as a sort of graduation from religion until we get married or die, something drastic like that; when what it signifies is that observance is supposed to start in earnest. That was certainly how my father took it. I went with him to the Minsker shule every morning for weeks, arising at an ungodly hour to drive there. Afterward he would drop me at the subway, and ride off to the messy building site for his day's aggravation and aging. It was hard going for both of us. It didn't last. Eventually I was rushing through morning prayers at home, in an abbreviated format which my sons have irreverently dubbed "Straps on, straps off," and which is the way they still do it, so far as I know. I don't inquire.

This chapter is about the story in the *Bronx Home News,* but since I've wandered this far afield, let me add one thing more. The drop from the packed bar-mitzva Sabbath to the meager little service Sunday morning was in retrospect the crux of the experience. If Pop hadn't made the effort I'd have missed the whole point. Anybody can stage a big bar mitzva, given a bundle of money and a boy willing to put up with the drills for the sake of the wingding. The backbone of our religion—who knows, perhaps of all religions in this distracted age—is a stubborn handful in a nearly vacant house of worship, carrying it on for just one more working day; out of habit, loyalty, inertia, superstition, sentiment, or possibly true faith; who can be sure which? My father taught me that somber truth. It has stayed with me, so that I still haul myself to synagogues on weekdays, especially when it rains or snows and the minyan looks chancy.

Herman Wouk

I MAGINE a building divided into many rooms. The building may be large or small. Every wall of every room is covered with pictures of various sizes; perhaps they number many thousands. They represent in color bits of nature—animals in sunlight or shadow, drinking, standing in water, lying on the grass; near to, a Crucifixion by a painter who does not believe in Christ; flowers; human figures sitting, standing, walking. . . . All this is carefully printed in a book—name of artist—name of picture. People with these books in their hands go from wall to wall, turning over pages, reading the names. Then they go away, neither richer nor poorer than when they came, and are absorbed at once in their business, which has nothing to do with art. Why did they come? In each picture is a whole lifetime imprisoned, a whole lifetime of fears, doubts, hopes, and joys.

Wassily Kandinsky

N EVER before had [Bishop Cheverus] undertaken such a journey, and all the courage of an apostle was necessary to support one under its fatigues and difficulties. A dark forest, no traces of road, briers and thorns, through which they were sometimes obliged to open themselves a path, and then, after many hours of fatigue, no nourishment but the morsel of bread they had carried with them. At night, their only bed some branches of trees spread on the ground, around which large fires must be kept lighted, in order to keep off serpents and other dangerous animals, that might have come to destroy them during their sleep. They travelled thus for several days, when, one morning (it was Sunday), they heard many voices singing in harmonious concert at a distance. M. Cheverus listened, then went on, and, to his great astonishment, discovered it to be a well-known chant, the royal Mass of Dumont, with which the great churches and cathedrals of France are wont to ring during their most solemn celebrations. What a delightful surprise, and what tender emotions his heart experienced! He felt it to be a scene at once affecting and sublime; for what could be more affecting than to see a people, and that a savage people, who had been destitute of a priest for 50 years, and yet were not the less faithful in celebrating the Lord's day; and what more sublime than the sacred chants, led by piety alone, responding afar in this immense and majestic forest, repeated by J. Huen-Dubourg   every echo, while they were borne to heaven by every heart?

THE churchwomen all bring flowers for the altar; they haul in arrangements as big as hedges, of wayside herbs in season, and flowers from their gardens, huge bunches of foliage and blossoms as tall as I am, in vases the size of tubs, and the altar still looks empty, irredeemably linoleum, and beige. We had a wretched singer once, a guest from a Canadian congregation, a hulking blond girl with chopped hair and big shoulders, who wore tinted spectacles and a long lacy dress, and sang, grinning, to faltering accompaniment, an entirely secular song about mountains. Nothing could have been more apparent than that God loved this girl; nothing could more surely convince me of God's unending mercy than the continued existence on earth of the church.

The higher Christian churches—where, if anywhere, I belong—come at God with an unwarranted air of professionalism, with authority and pomp, as though they knew what they were doing, as though people in themselves were an appropriate set of creatures to have dealings with God. I often think of the set pieces of liturgy as certain words which people have successfully addressed to God without their getting killed. In the high churches they saunter through the liturgy like Mohawks along a strand of scaffolding who have long since forgotten their danger. If God were to blast such a service to bits, the congregation would be, I believe, genuinely shocked. But in the low churches you can expect it any minute. This is the beginning of wisdom.   Annie Dillard

THE assumption of being an individual is our greatest limitation.   Pir Vilayat Khan

BEWARE, my body and my soul,
beware above all of crossing your arms
and assuming the sterile attitude of the spectator,
because life is not a spectacle.   Aimé Césaire

ONE of our great allies at present is the Church itself. Do not misunderstand me. I do not mean the Church as we see her spread out through all time and space and rooted in eternity, terrible as an army with banners. That, I confess, is a spectacle which makes our boldest tempters uneasy. But fortunately it is quite invisible to these humans. All your patient sees is the half-finished, sham Gothic erection on the new building estate. When he goes inside, he sees the local grocer with rather an oily expression of his face bustling up to offer him one shiny little book containing a liturgy which neither of them understands, and one shabby little book containing corrupt texts of a number of religious lyrics, mostly bad, and in very small print. When he gets to his pew and looks round him he sees just that selection of his neighbours whom he has hitherto avoided. You want to lean pretty heavily on those neighbours. Make his mind flit to and fro between an expression like "the body of Christ" and the actual faces in the next pew. It matters very little, of course, what kind of people that next pew really contains. You may know one of them to be a great warrior on the Enemy's side. No matter. Your patient, thanks to Our Father below, is a fool. Provided that any of those neighbours sing out of tune, or have boots that squeak, or double chins, or odd clothes, the patient will quite easily believe that their religion must therefore be somehow ridiculous.

C. S. Lewis

THE liturgical assembly is thus a theological corporation and each of its members a theologian whose discourse in faith is carried on not by concepts and propositions nearly so much as in the vastly complex vocabulary of experiences had, prayers said, sights seen, smells smelled, words said and heard and responded to, emotions controlled and released, sins committed and repented, children born and loved ones buried, and in many other ways no one can count or always account for. Their critical and reflective discourse is not merely about faith. It is the very way faith works itself out in the intricacies of human life both individually and in common. Its vocabulary is not precise, concise, or scientific. It is symbolic, aesthetic, ascetical, and sapiential. It is not just something she and her pastor think or say, but something they taste, the air they breathe. It is a sinuous discourse by which they and those innumerable millions like them, dead and born and yet unborn, work out the primary body of perceived data concerning what it really means when God pours . . . into the world as a member of our race. Nowhere else can that primary body of perceived data be read so well as in the living tradition of Christian worship.

Aidan Kavanagh

B ECAUSE of the central role of liturgical rites in disclosing within a community the important delineations and for presenting the mysterious holiness of God, the liturgical assembly will continue to be, as it has been for centuries, decisive for the church's self-understanding. It is in assembly that what the church knows to be true can and must be celebrated, and the very physical shape this public praise of the holy God takes will contribute to the slower work of theological reflection.

Mary Collins

L ITURGICAL prayer is not simply a confession of faith, whose only object is to define the area of dogma as precisely as possible, or to divide truth from error ever more sharply. It is rather that a spontaneous use is made, with God in view, of the deposit of faith; a joyful use of Revelation, in which at different times, among the fixed and basic facts, those traits are brought out which are nearest to the religious atmosphere, the experiences and interests of that period and people which has been the matrix of the liturgical prayer-formula.

Joseph Jungmann

T HE Christian faith has only one object, the mystery of Christ dead and risen. But this unique mystery subsists under different modes: It is prefigured in the Old Testament, it is accomplished historically in the earthly life of Christ, it is contained in mystery in the sacraments, it is lived mystically in souls, it is accomplished socially in the church, it is consummated eschatologically in the heavenly kingdom. Thus Christians have at their disposition several registers, a multidimensional symbolism, to express this unique reality. The whole of Christian culture consists in grasping the links that exist between bible and liturgy, gospel and eschatology, mysticism and liturgy. The application of this method to scripture is called exegesis; applied to liturgy it is called mystagogy. This consists in reading in the rites the mystery of Christ, and in contemplating beneath the symbols the invisible reality.

Jean Daniélou

THE theological principle operative here is one that was summarized so succinctly by Pius XII in *Mediator Dei:* The liturgy is the worship offered to the Father by the whole Christ, head and members. Thus, while the Mass may be a matter of individual believers fulfilling the wholesome duties of religion, or of a group of believers celebrating their faith and love, it is always something more: an act of the church as the Body of Christ. Furthermore, a sound theology of the liturgy will also emphasize the fact that what the church celebrates is not something devised of its own initiative, but a memorial entrusted to it by God. Hence the institution narrative in the eucharistic prayer, the assertion that the Lord's Prayer is "the prayer our Savior gave us," and the frequent references to the acts of God in such things as the nuptial blessing or the blessing of baptismal water. What all these point to is this: We do not "create" liturgy, we only attempt to celebrate as reverently and as faithfully as possible the sacred signs given us by God in Christ and passed down to us in elaborated forms by the Tradition. Thus, strictly speaking, when we celebrate the liturgy, it is not up to us what we do, nor is it actually we who celebrate: It is all done "through Christ our Lord."

There is, therefore, a certain irreducible "otherness" or "objectivity" to liturgical celebration which we do well to acknowledge, and this begins in the very act of assembling itself. The liturgical assembly is not another "audience" and the act of assembling is not just another process of arriving and taking places. The liturgy, we have said, is an act of the church—the church as realized in a local congregation—which is the Body of Christ. Thus, this assembled people is itself the primary sacrament of Christ, the outward and visible sign of the presence of Christ in and to the world, the medium of his own continuing mediatorship for the glorification of God and the sanctification of the human race.

Mark Searle

GOD could give us no greater gift than to establish as our Head the Word through whom God created all things and to unite us to that Head as members. The results are many. The Head is Son of God and Son of Man, one as God with the Father and one as a human being with us. When we speak in prayer to the Father, we do not separate the Son from the Father and when the Son's Body prays it does not separate itself from its Head. It is the one Savior of his Body, and Lord Christ Jesus, who prays for us and in us and who is prayed to by us. He prays for us as our priest, in us as our Head; he is prayed to by us as our God. Recognize therefore our own voice in him and his voice in us.

Augustine
Fifth century

To accomplish so great a work, Christ is always present in his church, especially in its liturgical celebrations. He is present in the sacrifice of the Mass, not only in the person of his minister, "the same now offering, through the ministry of priests, who formerly offered himself on the cross," but especially under the eucharistic elements. By his power he is present in the sacraments, so that when a person baptizes it is really Christ himself who baptizes. He is present in his word, since it is he himself who speaks when the holy scriptures are read in the church. He is present, lastly, when the church prays and sings, for he promised: "Where two or three are gathered together in my name, there am I in the midst of them" (Matthew 18:20).

Constitution on the
Sacred Liturgy

At Mass or the Lord's Supper, the people of God are called together, with a priest presiding and acting in the person of Christ, to celebrate the memorial of the Lord or eucharistic sacrifice. For this reason Christ's promise applies supremely to such a local gathering of the church: "Where two or three come together in my name, there am I in their midst" (Matthew 18:20). For at the celebration of Mass, which perpetuates the sacrifice of the cross, Christ is really present to the assembly gathered in his name; he is present in the person of the minister, in his own word, and indeed substantially and permanently under the eucharistic elements.

General Instruction of
the Roman Missal

THE Christian faithful are those who, inasmuch as they have been incorporated in Christ through baptism, have been constituted as the people of God; for this reason, since they have become sharers in Christ's priestly, prophetic and royal office in their own manner, they are called to exercise the mission which God has entrusted to the church to fulfill in the world, in accord with the condition proper to each one.

Code of Canon Law

AMONG the symbols with which liturgy deals, none is more important than this assembly of believers. It is common to use the same name to speak of the building in which those persons worship, but that is misleading. In the words of ancient Christians, the building used for worship is called domus *ecclesiae,* the house of the church.

The most powerful experience of the sacred is found in the celebration and the persons celebrating, that is, it is found in the action of the assembly: the living words, the living gestures, the living sacrifice, the living meal.

*Environment and Art
in Catholic Worship*

VERY good. Asherel, how shall we start? I do not want to, God forbid, hurt you or make you feel bad. I talk to you out of love for you and your dear parents." He paused. "I knew your grandfather in Russia. I was with him and the Rebbe's father the night he was killed. All the Jewish people are one body and one soul, he believed. If one part of the body hurts, the entire body hurts—and the entire body must come to the help of the part that hurts. Are you listening to me, Asher?"

I hurt, I thought. Who is coming to my help? "Yes," I said. "I am listening."

"Good," he said gently, and stroked his dark beard. "Asherel, your father also sees the Jewish people as one body and one soul. When a head hurts in the Ukraine, your father suffers in Brooklyn. When Jews cannot study Torah in Kiev, your father cannot sit still in Brooklyn. Do you understand me, Asherel?"

Chaim Potok

I F a poor man or a poor woman comes, whether they are from your own parish or from another, above all if they are advanced in years, and if there is no room for them, make a place for them, O bishop, with all your heart, even if you yourself have to sit on the ground.

You must not make any distinction between persons, if you wish your ministry to be pleasing before God.

When you are teaching, command and exhort the people to be faithful to the assembly of the church. Let them not fail to attend, but let them gather faithfully together. Let no one deprive the church by staying away; if they do, they deprive the body of Christ of one of its members.

The Didascalia of the Apostles
Second century

T O the bath and the table,
To the prayers and the word,
I call every seeking soul.

Inscription on a Bell

EVEN if you do not understand the meaning of the words, for the time being teach your mouth to say them, for the tongue is sanctified by the words alone whenever it says them with good will. Once we have become confirmed in this custom, we will not neglect this congenial duty either deliberately or through indifference, as custom will compel us to fulfill this grateful service every day, even if unwilling. Nor will any complaint concerning this singing arise, even if one has grown old, is still a child, has a rough voice, or is altogether ignorant of rhythm. This is because what is sought here is a sober soul, an alert mind, a contrite heart, sound reason and a clear conscience. If having these, you enter into the holy choir of God, you will be able to stand beside David yourself.

John Chrysostom
Fourth century

IT is fitting that you should live in harmony with the will of the bishop, as indeed you do. For your justly famous presbytery, worthy of God, is attuned to the bishop as the strings to a harp. Therefore by your concord and harmonious love Jesus Christ is being sung. Now do each of you join in this choir, that being harmoniously in concord you may receive the key of God in unison, and sing with one voice through Jesus Christ to the Father.

Ignatius of Antioch
First century

WHAT is more pleasing than a psalm? David himself puts it nicely: "Praise the Lord," he says, "for a psalm is good" (Psalm 146:1). And indeed! A psalm is the blessing of the people, the praise of God, the commendation of the multitude, the applause of all, the speech of every person, the voice of the church, the sonorous profession of faith, devotion full of authority, the joy of liberty, the noise of good cheer, and the echo of gladness. It softens anger, it gives release from anxiety, it alleviates sorrow; it is protection at night, instruction by day, a shield in time of fear, a feast of holiness, the image of tranquillity, a pledge of peace and harmony, which produces one song from various and sundry voices in the manner of a cithara. The day's dawning resounds with a psalm, with a psalm its passing echoes.

Ambrose
Fourth century

I n a sense, our liturgy is a higher form of silence. It is pervaded by an awed sense of the grandeur of God which resists description and surpasses all expression. The individual is silent. We do not bring forth our own words. Our saying the consecrated words is in essence an act of listening to what they convey. *The Spirit of Israel speaks, the self is silent.*

Twofold is the meaning of silence. One, the abstinence from speech, the absence of sound. Two, inner silence, the absence of self concern, stillness. One may articulate words with the voice and yet be inwardly silent. One may abstain from uttering any sound and yet be overbearing.

Both are inadequate: our speech as well as our silence. Yet there is a level that goes beyond both: the level of song. "There are three ways in which one expresses deep sorrow: the person on the lowest level cries; the person on the second level is silent; the person on the highest level knows how to turn sorrow into song." True prayer is a song.

Abraham Joshua
Heschel

I am not satisfied with those who despise music, as all fanatics do; for music is an endowment and a gift of God, not a gift of other persons. It also drives away the devil and makes people cheerful; one forgets all anger, unchasteness, pride, and other vices. I place music next to theology and give it the highest praise.

Martin Luther
Sixteenth century

NOT long ago, at a difficult time in my life, when my husband was recovering from surgery, I attended a drum ceremony with a Native American friend. Men and boys gathered around the sacred drum and sang a song to bless it. Their singing was high-pitched, repetitive, solemn, and loud. As they approached the song's end, drumming louder and louder, I realized that the music was also restorative; my two-day headache was gone, my troubles no longer seemed so burdensome.

I wondered how this loud, shrill, holy music, the indigenous song of those who have truly seen the Plains, could be so restful, while the Gregorian chant that I am just learning to sing can be so quiet, and yet as stirring as any drum. Put it down to ecstasy.

Kathleen Norris

REBBE David was known and liked for his exuberant, contagious joy. Prayer sent him into rapture; he turned even the lamentations into song.

He outlived his wife, four sons and three daughters. At seventy-three he was alone and in mourning. Yet he did not give in to sadness. To praise God, one must live, he said, and to live, one must enjoy life; one must enjoy life in spite of life.

Elie Wiesel

ALL desires and promises were already present in symphonic creation and the voice of human speaking, but they were veiled and ambiguous.

The Word incarnate was the herald of a new song, but it had to lead the human song of silence in order to break out into an Easter alleluia.

The Spirit has given to the church the eucharistic hymn, entrusting it with crossing and reconstituting the cosmos and humanity until the song of love finally reaches its fullness.

Joseph Gelineau

O the happiness of the heavenly alleluia, sung in security, in fear of no adversity! We shall have no enemies
in heaven, we shall never lose a friend. God's praises are
sung both there and here, but here they are sung in anxiety,
there, in security; here they are sung by those destined to
die, there, by those destined to live for ever; here they are
sung in hope, there, in hope's fulfillment; here they are sung
by wayfarers, there, by those living in their own country.

So let us sing now, not in order to enjoy a life of leisure, but in
order to lighten our labors. You should sing as wayfarers do —
sing, but continue your journey. Do not be lazy, but sing to   Augustine
make your journey more enjoyable. Sing, but keep going.   Fifth century

D o but so live that your heart may truly rejoice in God,
that it may feel itself affected with the praises of God,
and then you will find that this state of your heart will neither
want a voice nor ear to find a tune for a psalm. Everyone at
one time or other is able to sing in some degree; there are
some times and occasions of joy that make all people ready
to express their sense of it in some sort of harmony. The joy
that they feel forces them to let their voice have a part in it.

Those therefore that saith they want a voice or an ear to sing
a psalm mistake the case; they want that spirit that really
rejoices in God; the dullness is in the heart and not in the
ear; and when the heart feels a true joy in God, when it has
a full relish of what is expressed in the psalms, they will find
it very pleasant to make the motions of the voice express the
motions of the heart.

As singing is a natural effect of joy in the heart, so it has also   William Law
a natural power of rendering the heart joyful.   Eighteenth century

"SPEAKING to yourselves in psalms and hymns and spiritual songs, singing and making melody in your heart to the Lord" (Ephesians 5:19).

How should we interpret these words? Do they mean that when you are filled with the Spirit, you should then sing with your mouth and your heart? Or that if you wish to be filled with the Holy Spirit, you should first sing? Is the singing with mouth and heart, mentioned by the apostle, meant to be the consequence of being filled by the Spirit, or the means towards it?

The infusion of the Holy Spirit does not lie within our power. It come as the Spirit wishes. And when it comes, this infusion will so greatly animate the powers of our spirit that the song to God breaks out of itself. Freedom of choice lies only between leaving this song to be sung in the heart alone, or expressing it aloud for all to hear.

The words of the apostle must be taken in the second sense rather than the first. Desire to be filled with the Spirit, and sing with that aim in mind. Singing will set alight the Spirit.

Theophan
Eighth century

THE hand on the word,
    the hand in the midst
of the word for a God,
the hand on the measuring span,
on the waist of our spirits.

We must shake up the box of our language,
startle the vocables
till they circle like seagulls;
we must pound out
the mud like a batter
till it sings;
all must be soiled with our tears,
washed with our blood,
all take the violet's tint

till a river leaps forth,
the whole of a river
in the span of a tea-cup;
so goes the song:
that is the word
for a river.

Pablo Neruda

L EARN these tunes before you learn any others; afterwards learn as many as you please.

Sing them exactly as they are printed here, without altering or mending them at all; and if you have learned to sing them otherwise, unlearn it as soon as you can.

Sing all. See that you join with the congregation as frequently as you can. Let not a slight degree of weakness or weariness hinder you. If it is a cross to you, take it up, and you will find it a blessing.

Sing lustily and with a good courage. Beware of singing as if you were half dead, or half asleep; but lift up your voice with strength. Be no more afraid of your voice now, nor more ashamed of its being heard, than when you sang the songs of Satan.

Sing modestly. Do not bawl, so as to be heard above or distinct from the rest of the congregation, that you may not destroy the harmony; but strive to unite your voices together, so as to make one clear melodious sound.

Sing in time. Whatever time is sung be sure to keep with it. Do not run before nor stay behind it; but attend close to the leading voices, and move therewith as exactly as you can; and take care not to sing too slow. This drawling way naturally steals on all who are lazy; and it is high time to drive it out from us, and sing all our tunes just as quick as we did at first.

Above all sing spiritually. Have an eye to God in every word you sing. Aim at pleasing God more than yourself, or any other creature. In order to do this attend strictly to the sense of what you sing, and see that your heart is not carried away with the sound, but offered to God continually; so shall your singing be such as the Lord will approve here, and reward you when he cometh in the clouds of heaven.

John Wesley
Eighteenth century

W ITH the understanding that unity and harmony stood in opposition to duality and disharmony the primitive church rejected all heterophony and polyphony. The greatest possible harmony was pursued as the musical expression of the union of souls and of the community, as it prevailed in the early Christian liturgy. It is in this sense that the entire community of Christians, according to Clement of Alexandria, becomes a single symphonia:

> We want to strive so that we, the many, may be brought together into one love, according to the union of the essential unity. As we do good may we similarly pursue unity. . . . The union of many, which the divine harmony has called forth out of a medley of sounds and division, becomes one symphony, following the one leader of the choir and teacher, the Word, resting in that same truth and crying out: "Abba, Father. . . ."

The ideal of early Christian singing was unity or monophony. The most ancient evidence for this is probably found in the prefaces of the Mass, which speak of the angels and archangels, cherubim and seraphim, *qui non cessant clamare quotidie una voce dicentes: Sanctus, Sanctus, Sanctus Dominus Deus Sabaoth.*

Johannes Quasten

W HEN in our music God is glorified,
And adoration leaves no room for pride,
It is as though the whole creation cried Alleluia!

How often, making music, we have found
A new dimension in the world of sound,
As worship moved us to a more profound Alleluia!

So has the church in liturgy and song,
In faith and love, through centuries of wrong,
Borne witness to the truth in ev'ry tongue, Alleluia!

And did not Jesus sing a psalm that night
When utmost evil strove against the light?
Then let us sing, for whom he won the fight, Alleluia!

Let ev'ry instrument be tuned for praise!
Let all rejoice who have a voice to raise!
And may God give us faith to sing always Alleluia!   Fred Pratt Green

U NDOUBTEDLY the first human being was an artist. . . .

The necessity for dream is stronger than any utilitarian need.
In the language of science, the necessity for understanding
the unknowable comes before any desire to discover the
unknown.

The human being's first expression, like our first dream, was
an aesthetic one. Speech was a poetic outcry rather than a
demand for communication. Our original ancestors, shout-
ing consonants, did so in yells of awe and anger at their
tragic state, at their own self-awareness, and at their own
helplessness before the void. . . .

The human in language is literature, not communication.
Our first cry was a song. Our first address to a neighbor was
a cry of power and solemn weakness, not a request for a
drink of water.   Barnett Newman

P REFERENCE for the hierophanic entails doubt about the verbal, since the power of mystery cannot be expressed in
human language and the cosmos is more expressive of divine
awesomeness than is the human tongue.   David N. Power

THE sublime may be sensed in things of beauty as well as in acts of goodness and in the search for truth. The perception of beauty may be the beginning of the experience of the sublime. The sublime is that which we see and are unable to convey. It is the silent allusion of things to a meaning greater than themselves. It is that which all things ultimately stand for; "the inveterate silence of the world that remains immune to curiosity and inquisitiveness like distant foliage in the dusk." It is that which our words, our forms, our categories can never reach. This is why the sense of the sublime must be regarded as the root of our creative activities in art, thought, and noble living. Just as no flora has ever fully displayed the hidden vitality of the earth, so has no work of art, no system of philosophy, no theory of science, ever brought to expression the depth of meaning, the sublimity of reality in the sight of which the souls of saints, artists, and philosophers live.

Abraham Joshua Heschel

WHILE our words and art forms cannot contain or confine God, they can, like the world itself, be icons, avenues of approach, numinous presences, ways of touching without totally grasping or seizing. Flood, fire, the rock, the sea, the mountain, the cloud, the political situations and institutions of succeeding periods—in all of them Israel touched the face of God, found help for discerning a way, moved toward the reign of justice and peace. Biblical faith assures us that God covenants a people through human events and calls the covenanted people to shape human events. . . .

Quality is perceived only by contemplation, by standing back from things and really trying to *see* them, trying to let them speak to the beholder. Cultural habit has conditioned the contemporary person to look at things in a more pragmatic way: "What is it worth?" "What will it do?" Contemplation sees the hand stamp of the artist, the honesty and care that went into an object's making, the pleasing form and color and texture. Quality means love and care in the making of something, honesty and genuineness with any materials used, and the artist's special gift in producing a harmonious whole, a well-crafted work. This applies to music, architecture, sculpture, painting, pottery making, furniture making, as well as to dance, mime or drama—in other words, to any art form that might be employed in the liturgical environment or action.

Appropriateness is another demand that liturgy rightfully makes upon any art that would serve its action. The work of art must be appropriate in two ways: 1) it must be capable of bearing the weight of mystery, awe, reverence, and wonder which the liturgical action expresses; 2) it must clearly serve (and not interrupt) ritual action which has its own structure, rhythm and movement.

Environment and Art in Catholic Worship

L ITURGY happens only in the rough and tumbled landscape of spaces and times which people discover and quarry for meaning in their lives. This is an *artistic* enterprise. Liturgical repetition is thus a knowledgeable accomplishment, and its organization into definite rhythms of sounds, sights, gestures, and even smells is an act of human artistry—no more nor less so than building a house, composing a concerto, laying out a town, or playing cello. Therefore the student of liturgy must know not only heortology and history but the spatial, sonic, visual, and kinetic arts of ceremonial choreography as well. A liturgical scholar who is illiterate in the several human arts can never know his or her subject adequately.

Aidan Kavanagh

T HE only really effective apologia for Christianity comes down to two arguments, namely, the *saints* the church has produced and the *art* which has grown in its womb. Better witness is borne to the Lord by the splendor of holiness and art which have arisen in the community of believers than by the clever excuses which apologetics has come up with to justify the dark sides which, sadly, are so frequent

in the church's human history. If the church is to continue to transform and humanize the world, how can we dispense with beauty in our liturgies, that beauty which is so closely linked with love and with the radiance of the resurrection? No. Christians must not be too easily satisfied. They must make their church into a place where beauty—and hence truth—is at home. Without this the world will become the first circle of hell.

Joseph Ratzinger

B AD taste is the worst heresy.

Eric Gill

T HE special quality of beauty in crafts is that it is a beauty of intimacy. Since the articles are to be lived with every day, this quality of intimacy is a natural requirement. Such beauty establishes a world of grace and feeling. It is significant that in speaking of craft objects, people use terms such as savour and style. The beauty of such objects is not so much of the noble, the huge, or the lofty as the beauty of the warm and familiar. Here one may detect a striking difference between the crafts and the arts. People hang their pictures high up on walls, but they place their objects for everyday use close to them and take them in their hands.

Soetsu Yanagi

H OW can I buy the communion wine? Who am I to buy the communion wine? Someone has to buy the communion wine. Having wine instead of grape juice was my idea, and of course I offered to buy it. Shouldn't I be wearing robes and, especially, a mask? Shouldn't I *make* the communion wine? Are there holy grapes, is there holy ground, is anything here holy? There are no holy grapes, there is no holy ground, nor is there anyone but us. I have an empty knapsack over my parka's shoulders; it is cold, and I'll want my hands in my pockets. According to the Rule of St. Benedict, I should say, Our hands in our pockets. "All things come of thee, O Lord, and of thine own have we given thee." There must be a rule for the purchase of communion wine. . . .

Here is a bottle of wine with a label, Christ with a cork. I
bear holiness splintered into a vessel, very God of very God,
the sempiternal silence personal and brooding, bright on the
back of my ribs. I start up the hill.   Annie Dillard

THE dance is rigid down the aisle,
      a book embraced, held high, held dear:
the common carrier of the tales
on fiber come from cotton fields
and pulp from forest cut in Maine.
What earth has given hands have made
flat, thin and bound between two boards,
the pages covered now with marks
that image sounds that image all:
the pictures of pictures only
are letters gathered into words
and words lined up and bundled, tied—
yet here's the kernel of ourselves:
the poem, genealogies,
laws, letters, sayings, prophecies,
psalms, stories, visions handed on
from mouth to mouth and tongue to tongue
and page to page: a year or three
to tell it round again, this book
that dances now in incense sweet
and sweet its alphabet to kiss.   Gabe Huck

THE flesh is anointed
      that the soul might be consecrated."
Tertullian

"Oil for the athlete,
lotion for the bride."
Chrysostom

Oil applied ahead of time
seals the skin against its enemies—
sun and water, wind and cold;
gives the fighter a fighting chance
to slide and squirm elusively
evading capture and k.o.
Oil applied remedially
repairs the wounds of war and work,
chapped, cracked, broken skin
salved and soothed,
unguent for bruise and burn
for wound and rash
for scrage and scrofula. . . .
poured, smeared, daubed, rubbed in:
liniment of the spirit,
healing balm.

Oil for the athlete,
chrism for the bride;
oil for the sweatshop,
chrism for the ball;
oil for the first-aid-kit,
chrism for romance

Chrism is a beauty-oil:
sensuous lotion,
lovers' potion,
sign of the good times—
healthy glow, vitality and youth.
Heady-scent upon the sainted head,
fresh fragrance of the Lord's loved ones,
by the odor of whose unguents
Mark Searle   we are allured.

WHILE *the congregation sings a hymn of thanksgiving or an appropriate psalm, the celebrant kisses the altar and prays:* Remain in peace, O altar of God, and I hope to return to you in peace. May the sacrifice which I have offered upon you forgive my sins, help me to avoid faults and prepare me to stand blameless before the throne of Christ. I know not whether I will be able to return to you again to offer sacrifice. Guard me, O Lord, and protect your holy church, that it may remain the way of salvation and the light of the world. Amen.

Maronite rite

YOUR questions are, "What is essential?" and "How shall the greatest economy be practiced?"

Water runs down hill concisely. There is no quibbling about it. It does not have to run up hill in order to be entertaining. We have always followed its course with fascination. A human soul may reveal its mysteries through direct expression, simple speech, simple gesture, simple painting, just as the soul of the brook is expressed in full simplicity and economy.

One of the curses of art is "Art." This filling up of things with "decoration," with by-play, to make them "beautiful."

When art has attained a place, surfaces will be infinitely less broken. There will then be millions less of *things,* less words, less gesture, less of everything. But each word and each gesture and everything will count in a fuller value.

When we have attained a sense of the relative value of things, we will need fewer things. We will not change a line or form or color until we *have* to—and when we do make a change, a wealth of meaning will then fill the world from this new gesture.

Robert Henri

THUS, when—out of my delight in the beauty of the house of God—the loveliness of the many-colored gems has called me away from external cares, and worthy meditation has induced me to reflect, transferring that which is material to that which is immaterial, on the diversity of the sacred virtues: then it seems to me that I see myself dwelling, as it were, in some strange region of the universe which neither exists entirely in the slime of the earth nor entirely in the purity of Heaven; and that, by the grace of God, I can be transported form this inferior to that higher world.

Abbot Suger of
St. Denis
Twelfth century

O LORD, who bless those who bless you, and sanctify those who trust in you, save your people and bless your inheritance; safeguard the fullness of your church; sanctify those who love the beauty of your house; in return, raise them to glory by your divine power and do not forsake us who put our hope in you.

Orthodox liturgy

WHAT is this place where we are meeting?
Only a house, the earth its floor.
walls and a roof, sheltering people,
windows for light, an open door.
Yet it becomes a body that lives
when we are gathered here,
and know our God is near.

Words from afar, stars that are falling,
Sparks that are sown in us like seed:
names for our God, dreams, signs and wonders
sent from the past are all we need.

We in this place remember and speak
Again what we have heard:
God's free redeeming word.

And we accept bread at his table,
broken and shared, a living sign.
Here in this world, dying and living,
we are each other's bread and wine.
This is the place where we can receive
What we need to increase:
our justice and God's peace.

Huub Oosterhuis

I s there then any sense in planning churches? If the only
thing the workers can honestly do is to guide all created
things into the form of their surrender? A building is home
and shelter, but that which is demanded here is misery and
exile.

No, in the great and real sense there is indeed little purpose
for by ourselves we can build no churches: that, God must
do. But far beneath the exalted realm of true architecture lies
that other area where houses rise as temporary structures
which are little more than needy dug-outs or scanty shelters.
Such emergency buildings are our only possible accom-
plishments before God, waiting-rooms before God's threshold. They confess to the infinite need and they wait until God
transforms it. This is the honorable way to build churches:
before God begins to work.

Rudolf Schwarz

O NE of the first requisites of a tea-master is the knowledge of how to sweep, clean, and wash, for there is an
art in cleaning and dusting.

Okakura Kakuzo

THE house is inhabited, by a peculiar people doing peculiar things, making the house a peculiar place indeed. The peculiarities do not derive from similarities to what everyone else does, but from the dissimilarities. Choirs sing at dinner, the bath water is more like fire, the table is an altar of sacrifice, the tub is a womb and a tomb. The house is shot through with vertiginous peculiarities in whole and every part. It must be designed and built not to soften or wipe out its peculiarities but to intensify and sustain them. They are, after all, what make it what it is. . . .

The task of liturgy, architecture, theology and pastoral care lies in sustaining the dissimilarities between what the church does and what this world does. It is precisely in these dissimilarities that the mystery of God in Christ for the life of the world is discovered. We labor not to strengthen the family or secure justice but to stand before the living God in Christ in worship. When this happens, the human family is really strengthened and justice breaks out. But these are aftermaths rather than the purposes of the standing.

Ignoring this distinction, or getting it wrong, causes warps and reductionisms across the board—shopping mall architecture, loopy liturgy "for" this or that, sterile theology, and sentimental pastoral care preyed upon by political correctness. I maintain that better theology will not fix this any more than better architecture or a new tracker organ. Only liturgical discipline will, because in the liturgy done correctly, simply, lucidly, we stand in the undoubted presence of the Lover of our race, the Healer of our ills and lusts, the Relativiser of our politics, the Creator and Redeemer of all there is.

Aidan Kavanagh

IT is clear, therefore, that the lay congregation freely occupied the nave in Early Byzantine churches; moreover, they pressed with eagerness about the holiest parts of the church: the sanctuary barrier, ambo, and solea. Only the latter parts can be said to have been reserved for the use of the clergy. One cannot attribute any special "holiness" to the nave or to the space under the dome in the earliest domed plans of

Constantinople nor can one imagine that this space was meant to be viewed only in fragmentary fashion from the aisles and galleries. In Maximus' terminology, the faithful were already the initiates invited to the full revelation of the mysteries; all that was kept from them was the full import of the mysteries as they would be apprehended in heaven.

Thomas F. Mathews

HERE is born in Spirit-soaked fertility
a brood destined for another City,
begotten by God's blowing
and borne upon this torrent
by the church their virgin mother.
Reborn in these depths they reach for heaven's realm,
the born-but-once unknown by felicity.
This spring is life that floods the world,
the wounds of Christ its awesome source.
Sinner sink beneath this sacred surf
that swallows age and spits up youth.
Sinner here scour sin away down to innocence,
for they know no enmity who are by
one font, one Spirit, one faith made one.
Sinner shudder not at sin's kind and number,
for those born here are holy.

Baptistry inscription
Fifth century

WE shape our dwellings, and afterwards our dwellings
shape us.

Author unknown

IF you let your hand follow along the real walls of a gallery, eventually you will end up on the outside wall of the building. I began to think that the walls I made could also be continued: so from the inside of the gallery they could go to the entrance and from there outside to the external walls and then to the walls of the surrounding buildings. The space between the buildings could then become a space from which the work continued. Everything comes out from the inside; it is all connected. The gallery walls are connected to the exterior walls; the building walls are in a sense the location's inside walls; the location is part of a town; the town is part of the country. And so the circle widens. There is no limit.

Tadashi Kawamata

W ORSHIP within the context of the late antique and early medieval world was not merely a pious curiosity nor was it a discrete activity, one among many cultural or social events in the life of the city. Rather, it was an expression of the very heart of urban life, of the very meaning of the *civitas* as a holy place. The *domus ecclesiae* of the pre-Constantinian period may have become a *domus dei* in subsequent centuries, but the city itself became a house for the Christian assembly. It could even be conceived of as a *domus dei.* Chrysostom expressed this during the crisis of the Statues at Antioch by saying that in time of need ". . . the whole city has become church for us."

John Baldovin

Isamu Noguchi

T O search the final reality of stone beyond the accident of time, I seek the love of matter. The materiality of stone, its essence, to reveal its identity—not what might be imposed but something closer to its being. Beneath the skin is the brilliance of matter.

S PEAKING of hearing and seeing, Northrop Frye said that "the word listened to and acted upon is the starting point of a course of action: the visible object brings one to a respectful halt in front of it." I would hope that the halt in front of the work of art would accept every challenge it offered and acknowledge for all the arts, at the end, what Flannery O'Connor said of fiction, that it is concerned "with mystery that is lived; ultimate mystery as we find it embodied in the concrete world of sense experience." And then a talent for conviction brings the experience into the world of speaking and listening.

Denis Donoghue

A DMITTEDLY the arts do also constitute a danger for the liturgy. The social prayer of the people, for instance, finds expression in song; next this song is refined to a higher artistic standard within the competence only of skilled singers— and the people become condemned to silence. Then comes the final step when the singing is yet further elaborated till it becomes concert music, retaining indeed the religious texts, but utterly worldly in its spirit and ministering only to aesthetic tastes. Or take the Mass vestments of the priest: They become ornamented with fine embroidery. But to display the beauty of the pattern to the best advantage it becomes important to avoid creases. So the chasuble is made of stiff material and then, to give freedom to the arms, parts of it have to be cut away. And so arises a shape having very little resemblance to an enveloping garment. The altar, which is essentially a table, is equipped with an ornamental centre-piece displaying, for example, a picture of the saint here venerated. From this centre-piece of Romanesque art there develops the gothic folding tryptich; and from this in turn grows the colossal reredos of the baroque period, by which the essential features of the altar are disguised rather than emphasized.

In art there seems to be a kind of centrifugal force, a tendency to break loose from the holy foundation of humble divine worship and to become an end to itself.

Joseph A. Jungmann

THE artist has to be a bridge builder between the contemporary art world that surrounds us and our own worshiping needs. The artist has to be a bridge builder between the liturgical expressions of the past that form the very best of tradition and the prayer needs of the present. The artist also has to be the bridge builder between the realities of our secular society and the sacredness of our worship. It would seem impossible to me for anyone to fulfill that role without being a person of deep prayer and faith.

Rembert G. Weakland

THE charge against Jesus was not "This man is a social revolutionary," but "Behold, a glutton and a drunkard" (Matthew 11:19). Critics may ask, "With the world in the shape it's in, why do your disciples build churches, carillons, stained-glass windows; pay for sculptors, musicians, painters; wear woven robes, drink from a hand-turned chalice, and place real flowers on their altars when plastic ones would do as well for less money?"

As Robert Hovda notes, it was the devil, rather than a prophet, who tried to convince Jesus that we live by bread alone; anything else, according to Satan, is sinful excess. The devil said this to one much poorer than I, living in a world more tragic than mine. Jesus' rebuke suggests that, for him, bread alone is not the sole justice issue.

William Willemon

FAITH grows when it is well expressed in celebration. Good celebrations foster and nourish faith. Poor celebrations may weaken and destroy it.

To celebrate the liturgy means to do the action or perform the sign in such a way that its full meaning and impact shine forth in clear and compelling fashion. Since liturgical signs are vehicles of communication and instruments of faith, they must be simple and comprehensible. Since they are directed to fellow human beings, they must be humanly attractive.

Music in Catholic Worship

FOR art in itself, in its role as art, the "meaning stops here." It is a reality in itself, for itself. Whether it be a classic painting or sculpture, an ordinary object rendered into art, an assemblage of stray objects, we look at it as it is, as it presents itself. The event of our encounter is for itself, a significant enjoyment, an experience of seeing, here, at this moment. And we are deepened, refreshed, challenged to reorder ourselves, to see in a new way our world and ourselves—we are re-created. Here is a point, an end, a stopping place. . . .

This is the first and utterly essential role of art and the artistic: to re-create ordinary experience into value, into enhanced experience; to provide the ends—the deep, immediate, present enjoyments—for which all instruments exist and from which alone they receive their point. When an event that we label art thus stops the heedless flow of time in an enhanced moment, a moment of new awareness or understanding, a moment of intense seeing and participation in what is seen, then (as the Zen tradition has taught us) the transcendent appears through art, and art and religion approach one another.

Langdon B. Gilkey

LONG long with wonder I thought you human,
almost beyond humanity but not.
Once, years ago, only in a high bare hall
of the great Catalan museum over Barcelona,
    I thought you might be more—

a Pantocrator glares down, from San Clemente de Tahull,
making me feel you probably were divine,
but not human, through that majestic image.
Now I've come on something where you see both—
    a photograph of it only—

Burgundian, of painted & gilt wood,
life-size almost (not that we know your Semitic stature),
attenuated, your dead head bent forward sideways,
your long feet hanging, your thin long arms out
    in unconquerable beseeching—

John Berryman

A RT is not only the revealer of the infinite: It is the very means of penetrating into it.

Charles Morice

T HE singers who sing not only with words, but also with understanding may greatly benefit not only themselves but those who hear them. Blessed David, making music in this way for Saul, was himself well pleasing to God. He drove away from Saul the troubled and frenzied disposition, making his soul calm. Similarly, liturgists who are able to sing in this way are summoning the souls of the people into tranquillity, and calling them into harmonious accord with those who form the heavenly chorus. Psalms are not recited with melodies merely to make pleasant sounds. Rather, this is a sure sign of the harmony of the soul's reflections. Indeed, the melodic psalmody is a symbol of the mind's well-ordered and undisturbed condition. The praising of God in well-tuned cymbals and harp and ten-stringed instrument was again a figure and sign of the parts of the body coming into natural concord like harp strings. When this happens, the thoughts of the soul become like cymbals. Body and soul then live and move and have their being in unity together through this grand sound, as if through the command of the Spirit, so, as it is written, one overcomes the dying of the body through life in the Spirit. One who sings praise beautifully brings rhythm to the soul. By this means one leads the soul from disproportion to proportion. The result is that the encouraged soul loses fear, thinks on good things, and embraces the future. Gaining composure by the singing of praises, the soul transcends the life of passions, and joyfully beholds according to the mind of Christ the most excellent thoughts.

Athanasius
Fourth century

A T the most basic level we humans act both timelessly and historically. The potter is no different. She works at her craft in a particular time and place. Yet where her time intersects with history, there is of necessity something that the potter wishes to "say," something that speaks both to her time and to her tradition. That "something," I would assert, must be personal, beautiful, and lasting.

My person is in the pot by reason of my shaping hands and my intentionality. Every pot is the result of a decision to modify nature according to what I think, feel, and know. I must take responsibility for my work. The word may be a bit grandiose, but there is an *ethic* involved in artistic creation, since what I do communicates itself for better or worse to others.

It is every artisan's hope that what is produced will be considered beautiful both in its function and in its being. For the potter who creates the most utilitarian objects—cups, vases, bowls, teapots—there is a constant challenge (and opportunity) to put beauty into work. This is our modest way of reaffirming the beauty of the large creation. "Beauty will save the world," says Father Zosima in *The Brothers Karamazov,* and in that rather large task of world salvation the artist plays a modest but real role: to create epiphanies of beauty in the mundane surroundings of everyday life.

Cecilia Davis
Cunningham

So the sermon hymn comes to a close with a somewhat unsteady amen, and the organist gestures the choir to sit down. Fresh from breakfast with his wife and children and a quick runthrough of the Sunday papers, the preacher climbs the steps to the pulpit with his sermon in hand. He hikes his black robe up at the knee so he will not trip over it on the way up. His mouth is a little dry. He has cut himself shaving. He feels as if he has swallowed an anchor. If it weren't for the honor of the thing, he would just as soon be somewhere else. . . .

The preacher pulls the little cord that turns on the lectern light and deals out his note cards like a riverboat gambler. The stakes have never been higher. Two minutes from now he may have lost his listeners completely to their own thoughts, but at this minute he has them in the palm of his hand. The silence in the shabby church is deafening because everybody is listening to it. Everybody is listening including even himself. Everybody knows the kind of things he has told them before and not told them, but who knows what this time, out of the silence, he will tell them?

Let him tell them the truth. Before the gospel is a word, it is silence. It is the silence of their own lives and of his life. It is life with the sound turned off so that for a moment or two you can experience it not in terms of the words you make it bearable by but for the unutterable mystery that it is. Let him say, "Be silent and know that I am God, saith the Lord" (Psalm 40:10). Be silent and know that even by my silence and absence I am known. Be silent and listen to the stones cry out.

Out of the silence let the only real news come, which is sad news before it is glad news and that is fairy tale last of all. The preacher is not brave enough to be literally silent for long, and since it is his calling to speak the truth with love, even if he were brave enough, he would not be silent for long because we are none of us very good at silence. It says too much. So let him use words, but, in addition to using them to explain, expound, exhort, let him use them to evoke, to set us dreaming as well as thinking, to use words as at their most prophetic and truthful, the prophets used them to stir in us memories and longings and intuitions that we starve for without knowing that we starve. Let him use words which do not only try to give answers to the questions that we ask or ought to ask but which help us to hear the questions that we do not have words for asking and to hear the silence that those questions rise out of and the silence that is the answer to those questions. Drawing on nothing fancier than the poetry of his own life, let him use words and images that help make the surface of our lives transparent to the truth that lies deep within them, which is the wordless truth of who we are and who God is and the gospel of our meeting.

Frederick Buechner

I know that many men and even women are afraid and angry when women do speak, because in this barbaric society, when women speak truly they speak subversively—they can't help it: If you're underneath, if you're kept down, you break out, you subvert. We are volcanoes. When we women offer our experiences as our truth, as human truth, all the maps change. There are new mountains.

That's what I want—to hear you erupting. You young Mount St. Helenses who don't know the power in you—I want to hear you. I want to listen to you talking to each other and to us all: whether you're writing an article or a poem or a letter or teaching a class or talking with friends or reading a novel or making a speech or proposing a law or giving a judgment or singing the baby to sleep or discussing the fate of nations, I want to hear you. Speak with a woman's tongue. Come out and tell us what time of night it is! Don't let us sink back into silence. If we don't tell our truth, who will? Who'll speak for my children, and yours?

Ursula K. Le Guin

ALL-SEEING Father of Christ,
hear now our prayers
and grace your minister
with a song of divine sweetness. . . .
Now draw near
and from this pure and sacred book
and in these God-inspired words
find sustenance for your soul
for here you shall behold the ministers of truth
proclaim the word of life
in a voice that pierces heaven itself.

Gregory Nazianzen
Fourth century

Italo Calvino   IT is not the voice that commands the story, it is the ear.

THE homily must above all be an integral part of the worship service. It is not "word"—rational discourse—in contrast to "sacrament"—symbolic, nonrational activity: the comprehensible providing the incomprehensible with interpretation or relief. Homilies, like liturgy generally, are reflections upon, expansions of, the biblical word. They are reasonable exercises because the word of God testified to in scripture is reasonable. The biblical word is not gibberish. It is not speech that transcends human categories, or oracular utterance that gives assurances no other speech can give. The biblical word is a record of the dialogue of believers with God, their report on all that deity has done for them and spoken to them and meant to them. The Bible is a people's speech to and about and with the God no human eye has seen. These holy books help us carry on a conversation

Gerard S. Sloyan   with the one who is life and all to us.

BE careful of simple words said often.

"Amen" makes demands
like an unrelenting schoolmaster:
fierce attention to all that is said;
no apathy, no preoccupation, no prejudice permitted.
"Amen":   We are present. We are open.
           We hearken. We understand
           Here we are; we are listening to your word.

"Amen" makes demands
like a signature on a dotted line:
sober bond to all that goes before;
no hesitation, no half-heartedness, no mental
     reservation allowed.
"Amen":   We support. We approve.
          We are of one mind. We promise.
          May this come to pass. So be it.

Be careful when you say "Amen."   Barbara Schmich

THOSE who run precipitately through the liturgy, rushing in and out of the prayer-texts, as if the task were to cover a maximum of space in a minimum of time, will derive little from worship. To be able to pray is to know how to stand still and to dwell upon a word. This is how some worshipers of the past would act: "They would repeat the same word many times, because they loved and cherished it so much that they could not part from it."

"The worshiper must direct the heart to each and every word, like one who walks in a garden collecting roses and rare flowers, plucking them one by one, in order to weave a garland. So the worshiper moves from letter to letter, from word to word, uniting them in prayer. Every word seized hold of me and cleaves to the soul, and entreats me not to abandon it, not to break their bond, saying: *Consider my light, my grace, my splendor. Am I not the word 'Baruch' (Blessed)? Hearken to me when you pronounce me. Consider me when you utter me.*"   Abraham Joshua Heschel

INDEED, there can be no prayer without a sense for the dignity of words, without a degree of deference to what they stand for.

In acts of genuine expression, what goes on between the soul and the word of prayer is more than an act of employment, of using words as if they were tools. Here the soul and the word react upon each other; the word is a creative force.

Words are not made of paper. Words of prayer are repositories of the spirit. It is only after we kindle a light in the words that we are able to behold the riches they contain. It is only after we arrive within a word that we become aware of the riches our own souls contain. . . .

Unless we understand that the word is stronger than the will; unless we know how to approach a word with all the joy, the hope or the grief we own, prayer will hardly come to pass. The words must not fall off our lips like dead leaves in the autumn. They must rise like birds out of the heart into the vast expanse of eternity. . . . In our own civilization, in which so much is being done for the cause of the liquidation of language, the realm of prayer is like an arsenal for the spirit, where words are kept clean, holy, full of power to inspire and to keep us spiritually alive.

Abraham Joshua
Heschel

WORDS strain,
Crack and sometimes break, under the burden,
Under the tension, slip, slide, perish,
Decay with imprecision, will not stay in place,
Will not stay still. Shrieking voices
Scolding, mocking, or merely chattering,
Always assail them.

T. S. Eliot

WE cannot apprehend something without attaching a meaning to it. We conceive of things by giving them names. For example, *soil* and *stone*. We cannot conceive of soil or stone unless we use these names. However hard you may try to remove the extra meanings, inevitably some meanings remain attached. There is no fire or water that exists as a phenomenon in the pure sense: There are images of fire and images of water that have been produced by humanity. Humankind actualizes reality by speaking about it.

Toshikatsu Endo

EVERYTHING must have a title not
naming is not understanding
not that understanding gives any title
to that which the meaning keeps wanting to mean

but as with any cradled infant better
have a name for it the fairies
bring or witches may not know
until he makes a name for herself later

and everybody calls it by it
and the wolves open their mouths in the woods
since form is everything the sense is sensing
ready to begin talking or has just fallen still

form is everything needed for silence to have anything to say.   Robert Kelly

WE put thirty spokes together and call it a wheel;
But it is on the space where there is nothing that
the utility of the wheel depends.
We turn clay to make a vessel;
But it is on the space where there is nothing that
the utility of the vessel depends.
We pierce doors and windows to make a house;
and it is on these spaces where there is nothing that
the utility of the house depends.
Therefore, just as we take advantage of what is, we should
recognize the utility of what is not.   Lao Tse

SILENCE is an instrument that plays in many keys, is appropriate to many moods. What all good forms of silence have in common is that they lead us to the point where we discover the limitations of speech and action, that point which is the threshold of mystery. The term "mystery" itself derives from a profoundly ancient word which probably meant covering one's mouth, thus being silent before that of which human language cannot speak. "Let us prepare ourselves to celebrate these sacred mysteries."

Mark Searle

WHAT does the word yiyaw mean?" I asked. "I saw it in the prayerbook. Am I saying it right? Yiyaw?"

"I don't ever remember seeing a word like that, Ilana," David said, "Where is it?"

"I saw it a lot of times. Maybe I'm not saying it right. I was reading slowly to myself because I can't follow everyone else, and I kept seeing these same two letters. I think you say them—"

"Oh," David interrupted. "Wait!"

"Don't say it!" one of his friends said loudly. "It's the name of God!"

"It's pronounced Adonoi when you pray," David said. "And you say HaShem when you're just using it in talk. You never pronounce those letters as they're written, Ilana."

"Why not?"

"The name of God is too holy to be pronounced."

"I don't understand."

"She doesn't understand," one of his friends echoed.

"That's the law," David said. "That's the way you're supposed to say it."

Chaim Potok

FOLLOW, poet, follow right
To the bottom of the night,
With your unconstraining voice
Still persuade us to rejoice;

With the farming of a verse
Make a vineyard of the curse,
Sing of human unsuccess
In a rapture of distress;

In the deserts of the heart
Let the healing fountain start,
In the prison of his days
Teach the free man how to praise.

W. H. Auden

PRAYER the Churches banquet, Angels age,
Gods breath in man returning to his birth,
The soul in paraphrase, heart in pilgrimage,
The Christian plummet sounding heav'n and earth;

Engine against th' Almightie, sinners towre,
Reversed thunder, Christ-side-piercing spear,
The six-daies world-transposing in an houre,
A kinde of tune, which all things heare and fear;

Softnesse, and peace, and joy, and love, and blisse,
Exalted Manna, gladnesse of the best,
Heaven in ordinarie, man well drest,
The milkie way, the bird of Paradise,

Church-bels beyond the starres heard, the soul bloud,
the land of spices; something understood.

George Herbert
Seventeenth century

MY God, my God, thou are a direct God, may I not say a literal God, a God that wouldst be understood literally and according to the plain sense of all that thou sayest? but thou are also (Lord, I intend it to thy glory, and let no profane misinterpreter abuse it to thy diminution), thou are a figurative, a metaphorical God too; a God in whose words there is such a height of figures, such voyages, such peregrinations to fetch remote and precious metaphors, such extensions, such spreadings, such curtains of allegories, such third heavens of hyperboles, so harmonious elocutions, so retired and so reserved expressions, so commanding persuasions, so persuading commandments, such sinews even in thy milk, and such things in thy words, as all profane authors seem of the seed of the serpent that creeps, thou art the Dove that flies.

John Donne
Seventeenth century

THE auditory imagination [is] the feeling for syllable and rhythms, penetrating far below the conscious levels of thought and feeling, invigorating every word; sinking to the most primitive and forgotten, returning to the origin and bringing something back, seeking the beginning and the end. It works through meanings, certainly, or not without meanings in the ordinary sense, and fuses the old and obliterated and the trite, the current, and the new and surprising, the most ancient and the most civilized mentality.

T. S. Eliot

LENGTHY explanations are always abnormal and should never occur as an immediate prelude to the act itself. The assembly needs sustained preparation and formation of various sorts—evangelical, homiletical, catechetical, and ascetical. It is when these are lacking that last-minute recourse is had on the part of slothful ministers to verbose explanations of what is about to happen. The risk this runs is that of turning the liturgy into a "learning experience," as it is called. In a culture such as ours the educational temptation is difficult to resist. But liturgy which is stylish and effective in incrementing *logos* leads not to the brink of clarity but to the edge of chaos. It deals not with the abolition of ambiguity but with the dark and hidden things of God. When it comes to liturgy, precision can be bought at too high a price, and some things cannot be said.

Aidan Kavanagh

RITUAL, symbol, sacrament and sacrifice all have a two-fold quality, which closely parallels our human situation. In their living state they have an outside and inside, a visible action and an invisible action, both real, both needed, and so closely interdependent that each loses its true quality if torn apart; for indeed an idolatry which pins religion to abstract thoughts and notions alone is not much better than an idolatry which pins it to concrete stocks and stone alone. Either of these extremes are impoverishments, which destroy the true quality of a full and living cultus, wherein spirit and sense must constantly collaborate, as they do in all our significant acts and experiences. Incited by God, dimly or sharply conscious of the obscure pressure of God, we respond to God best not by a simple movement of the mind, but by a rich and complex action, in which our whole nature is concerned, and which has at its full development the characters of a work of art. We are framed for an existence which includes not only thought and speech, but gesture and manual action; and when we turn Godward, our life here will not be fully representative of our nature, nor will our act of worship be complete, unless all these forms of expression find a place in it. Our religious action must be social as well as personal, rhythmic and ceremonial as well as interior and free. It must link every sense with that element of our being which transcends and coordinates sense, so that the whole of our nature plays its part in our total response to the Unseen. Therefore those artistic creations, those musical sounds and rhythmic movements which so deeply satisfy the human need for expressive action, must all come in, and the most ancient and primitive levels of our mental life be allowed to cooperate in our acts of adoration, no less than those more recent achievements of the race on which we prefer to dwell.

Evelyn Underhill

G OD hates the worship of the mere lips; God requires the worship of the heart. A person may bow and kneel and look religious, but he is not at all the nearer heaven, unless he tries to obey God in all things, and to do his duty. But if he does honestly strive to obey God, then his outward manner will be reverent also; decent forms will become natural to him; holy ordinances, though coming to him from the church, will at the same time come (as it were) from his heart; they will be part of himself, and he will as little think of dispensing with them as he would dispense with his ordinary apparel, nay, as he could dispense with tongue or hand in speaking or doing. This is the true way of doing devotional service; not to have feelings without acts, or acts without feelings; but both to do and to feel—to see that our hearts and bodies are both sanctified together, and become one; the heart ruling our limbs, and making the whole person serve God, who has redeemed the whole person, body as well as soul.

John Henry Newman
Nineteenth century

T HE Spirit begins this work in us and with us, not faced with the raw, passive earth out of which was fashioned the first Adam, or, much less, the virginal earth, permeated by faith, which was used in effecting the conception of the second Adam. What the Spirit finds is a remnant of glory, an icon of the Son: ceaselessly loved, but broken and disfigured. Each of us can whisper what the funeral liturgy cries out in the name of the dead person: "I remain the image of your inexpressible glory, even though I am wounded by sin!" This trust that cannot be confounded and this covenant that cannot be broken form the space wherein the patient mystery of our divinization is worked out. . . .

The liturgy is the great river into which all the energies and manifestations of the mystery flow together, ever since the very body of the Lord who lives with the Father has been ceaselessly "given up" to human beings in the church in order that they may have life. The liturgy is not something static, or a mental memorial, a model, a principle of action, a form of self-expression, or an escape into angelism. It reaches far beyond the signs in which it manifests itself and the effectiveness it contains. It is not reducible to its celebrations, although it is indivisibly contained in them. It finds expression in the human words of God that are written in the Bible and sung by the church, but these never exhaust it. It is at home in all cultures and not reducible to any of them. It unites the multitude of local churches without causing them to lose their originality. It feeds all the children of God, and it is in them that it ceaselessly grows. Although it is constantly being celebrated, it is never repeated but is always new.

Jean Carbon

S OME years ago, I spent an afternoon caught up in a piece of sewing I was doing. The waste basket near my sewing machine was filled with scraps of fabric cut away from my project. This basket of discards was a fascination to my daughter, Annika, who, at the time was three years old. She rooted through the scraps searching out the long bright strips of cloth, collected them to herself, and went off. When it had been silent too long, I took a moment to check on her and tracked her whereabouts to the back garden. I found her there, sitting in the grass with a long pole she had gotten from the garage. She was fixing the scraps to the top of the pole with great sticky wads of tape. Mothers sometimes ask foolish questions, and I asked one. I asked her what she was doing. Without taking her eyes from her work she said, "I'm making a banner for a precession [sic]. I need a precession so that God will come down and dance with us." With that, she solemnly lifted her banner to flutter in the wind, and slowly she got up to dance.

Gertrud Mueller
Nelson

THE liturgy of the eucharist, performed in all its brilliance and complexity, gave meaning to the new architecture in a concrete and very tangible fashion that affected the public as active participants rather than as mere spectators. The Christian in Early Byzantine times was less interested in the abstract symbolic possibilities of architectural forms than in the very real symbolic action which was entrance into divine life. The architecture was primarily designed to accommodate this mystical event, and other symbolism must always have been subordinated to this purpose. . . .

The First Entrance involved the participation not only of the clergy but of the entire congregation, accompanying the bishop with singing as they flooded into the church. The reading of the gospel required of the deacon not just his appearance before the doors to read, but an exciting procession to and from the ambo with the faithful crowding about him. The Entrance of the Mysteries represented not a simple transfer of gifts from a neighboring chapel to the main altar, but a true entrance or bringing-in of the gifts from a skeuophylakion placed outside the church itself. Communion was received by much larger numbers in the early liturgy, and the ceremony concluded not with the disappearance of the clergy within the sanctuary, but with the celebrant's processional return down the solea and through the nave of the church.

Thomas F. Matthews

N EXT the priest says: "Holy things to the holy." Holy are the offerings after they have received the visitation of the Holy Spirit; and you are holy after you have been privileged to receive the Holy Spirit. So things and persons correspond: Both are holy. Next you say: "One is holy, one is the Lord, Jesus Christ." For truly One only is holy—holy, that is, by nature; yet we are also holy, not, indeed, by nature, but by participation, training and prayer.

After this you hear the chanter inviting you with a sacred melody to communion in the holy mysteries, in the words: "O taste and see that the Lord is good." Entrust not the judgment to your bodily palate, but to unwavering faith. For in tasting you taste, not bread and wine, but the antitypical body and blood of Christ.

Coming up to receive, therefore, do not approach with your wrists extended or your fingers splayed, but making your left hand a throne for the right (for it is about to receive a King) and cupping your palm, so receive the Body of Christ; and answer "Amen." Carefully hallow your eyes by the touch of the sacred body, and then partake, taking care to lose no part of it. Such a loss would be like a mutilation of your own body. Why, if you had been given gold-dust, would you not take the utmost care to hold it fast, not letting a grain slip through your fingers, lest you be by so much the poorer? How much more carefully, then, will you guard against losing so much as a crumb of that which is more precious than gold or precious stones!

After partaking of the body of Christ, approach also the chalice of his blood. Do not stretch out your hands, but, bowing low in a posture of worship and reverence as you say, "Amen," sanctify yourself by receiving also the blood of Christ. While it is still warm on your lips, moisten your fingers with it and so sanctify your eyes, your forehead, and other organs of sense. Then wait for the prayer and give thanks to the God who has deigned to admit you to such high mysteries.

St. Cyril of Jerusalem
Fourth century

WHAT is procession?
Movement from place to place,
measured movement, stately movement,
a representative few treading a representative distance:
journey distilled.
This is what all journeys are, it proclaims,
this is journey at its heart.

Again and again,
from week to week,
from age to age,
there is something of endings and beginnings;
of closing doors behind and opening those ahead,
of meeting and walking together.

What is procession? A journey, distilled.

From age to age, from east to west
we have skipped and limped and marched and run
and shuffled and strolled our various ways.
Our stories reverberate in measured tread.

From age to age, from east to west
our hurried feet have marked
the peaks and valleys, the sand and stone,
the mud, the grass, the dust,
the streams.
We pause in solemn pace to remember:
All ground is holy ground.
We come interiorly shoeless.

What is procession?
It is journey distilled—journey at its heart,
a gathering into one movement
of a church on the way:
a pilgrim people, a dusty, longing people,
yet walking with heads high;
knowing ourselves, showing ourselves
to be the royal nation, the holy people
won by the Son,
called by his word,
gathered around his table.
There we discover again,
from age to age, from east to west,
for all our journeys,
Janet Schlichting   the source, the ground, the companion, the way.

THOSE whose task it is to teach and educate will have
to ask themselves—and this is all decisive—whether
they themselves desire the liturgical act or, to put it plainly,
whether they know of its existence and what exactly it consists of and that it is neither a luxury nor an oddity, but a
matter of fundamental importance. Or does it, basically,

mean the same to them as to the parish priest of the late nineteenth century who said: "We must organize the procession better; we must see to it that the praying and singing is done better." He did not realize that he should have asked himself quite a different question: How can the act of walking become a religious act, retinue for the Lord progressing through the land, so that an "epiphany" may take place.   Romano Guardini

THEN the deacon cries aloud, "Receive ye one another; and let us kiss one another." Think not that this kiss ranks with those given in public by common friends. It is not such: This kiss blends souls one with another, and solicits for them entire forgiveness. Therefore this kiss is the sign that our souls are mingled together, and have banished all remembrance of wrongs. . . . The kiss therefore is reconciliation, and for this reason holy; as the blessed Paul has in his epistles urged: "Greet ye one another with a holy kiss"; and Peter, "with a kiss of charity."   Cyril of Jerusalem
Fourth century

WHEN the good news of the gospel is proclaimed, we stand up. Godparents stand when in the child's place they make the solemn profession of faith, children when they renew these promises at their first communion. Bridegroom and bride stand when they bind themselves at the altar to be faithful to their marriage vow. On these and the like occasions we stand up.

Even when we are praying alone, to pray standing may more forcibly express our inward state. The early Christians stood by preference. The "Orante," in the familiar catacomb representation, stands in her long flowing robes of a woman of rank and prays with outstretched hands, in perfect free-dom, perfect obedience, quietly attending to the word, and in readiness to perform it with joy.

We may feel at times a sort of constraint in kneeling. One feels freer standing up, and in that case standing is the right position. But stand up straight: not leaning, both feet on the ground, the knees firm, not slackly bent, upright, in control. Prayer made thus is both free and obedient, both reverent and serviceable.

Romano Guardini

THE principal thing is to stand with the mind in the heart before God, and to go on standing before God unceas-ingly day and night, until the end of life.

Theophany
Eighth century

MORE is involved than simply extending the language of theology. It is, rather, a matter of determining the struc-tures by which we have defined our relation to the world and responded to our apprehension of the manifestation of the divine. To do theology is not to know God in a particu-larly modern way, but to respond to God in the weight and structure and movement of a given language. The propo-sitional language of traditional theology is a great imagina-tive achievement and part of the discipline and nourishment of the human spirit. But it shapes thought by the specificities of its location (German as against English) and by the gen-erality of its form (the structured action of Indo-European grammar); neither of these aspects represents the whole of human experience. Things which are talked about are things of curiosity, of argumentative interest, but they are not oper-ative in our experience. It is only as the experience of the sacred becomes embodied, takes shape in those structures that can in turn shape the nervous system that they work rather than standing as specimens in a logical museum.

John W. Dixon, Jr.

AFTER situating herself on a huge flat-sided rock, Baby Suggs bowed her head and prayed silently. The company watched her from the trees. They knew she was ready when she put her stick down. Then she shouted, "Let the children come!" and they ran from the trees toward her.

"Let your mothers hear you laugh," she told them, and the woods rang. The adults looked on and could not help smiling.

Then "Let the grown men come," she shouted. They stepped out one by one from among the ringing trees.

"Let your wives and your children see you dance," she told them, and groundlife shuddered under their feet.

Finally she called the women to her. "Cry," she told them. "For the living and the dead. Just cry." And without covering their eyes the women let loose.

It started that way: laughing children, dancing men, crying women and then it got mixed up. Women stopped crying and danced; men sat down and cried; children danced, women laughed, children cried until, exhausted and riven, all and each lay about the Clearing damp and gasping for breath. In the silence that followed, Baby Suggs, holy, offered up to them her great big heart.

She did not tell them to clean up their lives or to go and sin no more. She did not tell them they were the blessed of the earth, its inheriting meek or its glorybound pure.

She told them that the only grace they could have was the grace they could imagine. That if they could not see it, they would not have it.

"Here," she said, "in this here place, we flesh; flesh that weeps, laughs; flesh that dances on bare feet in grass. Love it. Love it hard. Yonder they do not love your flesh. They despise it. They don't love your eyes; they'd just as soon pick 'em out. No more do they love the skin on your back. Yonder they flay it. And O my people they do not love your hands. Those they only use, tie, bind, chop off and leave empty. Love your hands! Love them. Raise them up and kiss them. Touch others with them, pat them together, stroke them on your face 'cause they don't love that either. *You* got to love it, *you!* And no, they ain't in love with your mouth.

Yonder, out there, they will see it broken and break it again. What you say out of it they will not heed. What you scream from it they do not hear. What you put into it to nourish your body they will snatch away and give you leavins instead. No, they don't love your mouth. You got to love it. This is flesh I'm talking about here. Flesh that needs to be loved. Feet that need to rest and to dance; backs that need support; shoulders that need arms, strong arms I'm telling you. And O my people, out yonder, hear me, they do not love your neck unnoosed and straight. So love your neck; put a hand on it, grace it, stroke it and hold it up. And all your inside parts that they'd just as soon slop for hogs, you got to love them. The dark, dark liver—love it, love it, and the beat and beating heart, love that too. More than eyes or feet. More than lungs that have yet to draw free air. More than your life-holding womb and your life-giving private parts, hear me now, love your heart. For this is the prize." Saying no more, she stood up then and danced with her twisted hip the rest of what her heart had to say while the others opened their mouths and gave her the music. Long notes held until the four-part harmony was perfect enough for their deeply loved flesh.

Toni Morrison

W HEN we cross ourselves, let it be with a real sign of the cross. Instead of a small cramped gesture that gives no notion of its meaning, let us make a large unhurried sign, from forehead to breast, from shoulder to shoulder, con-sciously feeling how it includes the whole of us, our thoughts, our attitudes, our body and soul, every part of us at once, how it consecrates and sanctifies us.

It does so because it is the sign of the universe and the sign of our redemption. On the cross Christ redeemed human-kind. By the cross he sanctifies us to the last shred and fiber of our being. We make the sign of the cross before we pray to collect and compose ourselves and to fix our minds and hearts and wills upon God. We make it when we finish pray-ing in order that we may hold fast the gift we have received from God. In temptations we sign ourselves to be strength-ened; in dangers, to be protected. The cross is signed upon us in blessings in order that the fullness of God's life may flow into the soul and fructify and sanctify us wholly.

Think of these things when you make the sign of the cross. It is the holiest of all signs. Make a large cross, taking time, thinking what you do. Let it take in your whole being—body, soul, mind, will, thoughts, feelings, your doing and not-doing—and by signing yourself with the cross strengthen and consecrate the whole in the strength of Christ, in the name of the triune God.   Romano Guardini

C HRISTIANS often ask why God does not speak to them, as they believed God did in former days. When I hear such questions, it always makes me think of the rabbi who was asked how it could be that God was often manifest to people in the olden days whereas nowadays nobody ever sees God. The rabbi replied, "Nowadays there is no longer anybody who can bow low enough."   Carl Jung

Z EDEKIAH was one and twenty years old when he began to reign. . . . And he did that which was evil in the sight of the Lord his God, and humbled not himself before Jeremiah the prophet speaking from the mouth of the Lord . . . but he stiffened his neck and hardened his heart from turning unto the Lord God Israel."

Unbending, unyielding,
unacknowledging of God or man.

Without a supple neck
how could I greet a neighbor in a crowd?
how could I tell my child she is doing well?
how could I express my grief and shame?

how could I assent without interrupting?
how could I show sadness in the face of suffering?
how could I show solidarity with one who speaks?
how could I offer my silent respect to a great lady?
how could I honor an eminent man?
how could I accept the verdict of my peers?
. . . simply, silently, wordlessly?

how could I surrender too the blessing
of the One who alone can deliver me out of death?

how could I acknowledge
that there is only one Name
by which I can be saved—
Mark Searle   the name of Jesus?

T HERE is no power of *li* if there is no learned and accepted
convention, or if we utter the words and invoke the
power of the convention in an inappropriate setting, or if the
ceremony is not fully carried out, of if the persons carrying
out the ceremonial roles are not those properly authorized
("authorization"—again a ceremony). In short, the pecu-
liarly moral yet binding power of ceremonial gesture and
word cannot be abstracted from or used in isolation from
ceremony. It is not a distinct power we happen to use in ceremony; it is the power *of* ceremony. . . .

The image of Holy Rite as a metaphor of human experience
brings foremost to our attention the dimension of the holy in
our existence. There are several dimensions of Holy Rite
which culminate in its holiness. Rite brings out forcefully not
only the harmony and beauty of social forms, the inherent
and ultimate dignity of human intercourse; it brings out also
the moral perfection implicit in achieving one's ends by
dealing with others as beings of equal dignity, as free copar-
ticipants in *li*. Furthermore, to act by ceremony is to be completely open to the other; for ceremony is public, shared,

transparent; to act otherwise is to be secret, obscure and devious, or merely tyrannically coercive. It is in this beautiful and dignified, shared and open participation with others who are ultimately like oneself that we realize ourselves. Thus perfect community becomes an inextricable part, the chief aspect, of divine worship—again an analogy with the central law taught by Jesus.

Herbert Fingarette

R ITES serve to shorten that which is too long and lengthen that which is too short, reduce that which is too much and augment that which is too little, express the beauty of love and reverence and cultivate the elegance of righteous conduct. Therefore, beautiful adornment and coarse sackcloth, music and weeping, rejoicing and sorrow, though pairs of opposites, are in the rites equally utilized and alternatively brought into play.

Hsun Tzu
Third century BCE

R ITES symbolize joyful and sad occasions but never turn joyful or sad themselves. They express love without passion, austerity without hardship, sorrow without grief. Rites articulate real life, they mold it into their restrictive forms but they never fully merge with it.

Louis Dupré

T HE liturgy, the dwelling place of present and remembered encounter with the living God, itself begins to think and speak for the assembly and turns wholly into music, not in the sense of outward, audible sounds, but by virtue of the power and momentum of its inward flow. Then, like the current of a mighty river polishing stones and turning wheels by its very movement, the flow of liturgical worship creates in passing, and by the force of its own laws, cadence and rhythm and countless other forms and formations, still more important and until now undiscovered, unconsidered, and unnamed.

What results from a liturgical act is not only "meaning," but an ecclesial transaction with reality, a transaction whose ramifications escape over the horizon of the present, beyond the act itself, to overflow even the confines of the local assembly into universality. The act both changes and outstrips the assembly in which it occurs. The assembly adjusts to that change, becoming different from what it was before the act happened. This adjustment means that subsequent acts of liturgy can never touch the assembly in exactly the same way as the previous act did. And it is in the constant adjustment to such change that an assembly increments its own awareness of its distinctive nature, that it shakes out and tests its own public and private norms of life and faith, that it works out its sustained response to the phenomenon of its own existence under God in the real world, a world whose source is the same as that of the assembly itself. It is all this which is the ecclesial society's fundamental and most important business. It is where church order, mission, morals, ministry, and theology are born. It is where all these, together with cosmology and evangelism, emerge in intimately related form, not yet separated out into competing and often contradictory endeavors which are by definition matters of the second order.

Aidan Kavanagh

A NAMNESIS" and "amnesia" come from a common Greek root. The biblical and liturgical use of the word "anamnesis" rises from a perception that there is a disorder analogous to clinical amnesia that plagues the human community. To be human is to be threatened with spiritual amnesia. At the level of our spiritual identity we do not remember for long who we really are. Those ultimate relationships that give us our spiritual identity slip from consciousness all too easily, and we lapse into noncomprehension about our deepest identity.

Corporate public ritual brings us together to participate actively in the relationships that identify us spiritually. Liturgical rites provide self-engaging activity of a symbolic form which points us to and engages us personally in the mystery within which we live. For it is both our faith and our experience that the mystery of Christ is always present. But it is equally our experience that we are inattentive to the truth of our origins and our destiny. We forget who we are, where we came from, where we are headed. So we assemble when it is timely to invest ourselves as a community of Christians in liturgical anamnesis. The self-engaging activity of our liturgy not only causes us to remember who we are; it invites us to commit ourselves to a life congruent with our identity. All liturgy is anamnesis.

Mary Collins

THE island where I live is peopled with cranks like myself. In a cedar-shake shack on a cliff—but we all live like this—is a man in his thirties who lives alone with a stone he is trying to teach to talk.

Wisecracks on this topic abound, as you might expect, but they are made as it were perfunctorily, and mostly by the young. For in fact, almost everyone here respects what Larry is doing, as do I, which is why I am protecting his (or her) privacy, and confusing for you the details. It could be, for instance, a pinch of sand he is teaching to talk, or a prolonged northerly, or any one of a number of waves. But it is, in fact, I assure you, a stone. It is—for I have seen it—a palm-sized oval beach cobble whose dark gray is cut by a band of white which runs around and, presumably, through it; such stones we call "wishing stones," for reasons obscure but not, I think, unimaginable.

He keeps it on a shelf. Usually the stone lies protected by a square of untanned leather, like a canary asleep under its cloth. Larry removes the cover for the stone's lessons, or more accurately, I should say, for the ritual or rituals which they perform together several times a day.

No one knows what goes on at these sessions, least of all myself, for I know Larry but slightly, and that owing only to a mix-up in our mail. I assume that like any other meaning-ful effort, the ritual involves sacrifice, the suppression of self-consciousness, and a certain precise tilt of the will, so that the will becomes transparent and hollow, a channel for the work. I wish him well. It is a noble work, and beats, from any angle, selling shoes.

Reports differ on precisely what he expects or wants the stone to say. I do not think he expects the stone to speak as we do, and describe for us its long life and many, or few, sensations. I think instead that he is trying to teach it to say a single word, such as "cup," or "uncle." For this purpose he has not, as some have seriously suggested, carved the stone a little mouth, or furnished it in any way with a pocket of air which it might then expel. Rather—and I think he is wise in this—he plans to initiate his son, who is now an infant liv-ing with Larry's estranged wife, into the work, so that it may continue and bear fruit after his death.

Annie Dillard

THE assembly, remembering Christ in a profound act of recollection, discovers its own mystery, its identity as the body of Christ in the world, continuing his surrender to God and to the work of God, until the end of time ("ready to greet him when he comes again").

Mark Searle

TAKE care and be earnestly on your guard not to forget the things which your own eyes have seen, nor let them slip from your memory as long as you live, but teach them to your children and your children's children.

Deuteronomy 4:9

TRADITION is not wearing your grandfather's hat; tradition is begetting a child.

Pablo Picasso

STEP by step, as I made my way back to church, I began to find that many of the things modern people assume are irrelevant—the liturgical year, the liturgy of the hours, the incarnation as an everyday reality—are in fact essential to my identity and my survival. I'm not denying the past, or trying to bring it back, but am seeking in my inheritance what theologian Letty Russell terms "a usable past." Perhaps I am also redefining frontier not as a place you exploit and abandon but as a place where you build on the past for the future. When we journey here, we discover it is no less old than new. T. S. Eliot wrote, "The end of all our exploring / Will be to arrive where we started / And know the place for the first time." Against all the odds, I rediscovered the religion I was born to, and found in it a home.
Kathleen Norris

SPIRIT," in the Christian sense of the word, does not mean just a purely interior feeling or idea. It means that, certainly, but it involves much more. "Spirit" always means, for Christians, some interior reality, but which tends toward incarnation, or rather cannot even exist without being incarnate. And it is not in the rubrics that the spirit of the liturgy has to take flesh, whatever may be their use and even necessity in leading us along the right path. It is in a general behavior, in a whole atmosphere; more deeply, it is in what we call an "ethos," a turn of mind and heart which is to pervade all the details of the ritual, so as to make of them a coherent embodiment of that "spirit" which is not just our spirit, but what this becomes when the Holy Spirit, the Spirit of God, is at work in us. . . .

Authentic Christianity lives only by tradition, not a tradition of dead formulae or mechanical practices, but a tradition of life, a life that is to grow organically, in and through some embodiment. In the continuity of its body, as well as in its ever renewed aspects, both the permanence and the ever creative power of the same Spirit have to be constantly manifested and exercised.
Louis Bouyer

THOSE of us who were deeply involved in historical, theological and pastoral consideration of the liturgy are, by this very fact, virtually incapable of leaving it alone. Loving it, we fondle it until it is misshapen. Certain that with a bit more planning it can be somehow "better" next Sunday than last, we deny the assembly one thing that it desperately needs: immersion in a ritual pattern whose authority, dimly understood but powerfully experienced, transcends our own ingenuity, erudition, and energy. At the risk of being hoist on my own petard, I must confess that we need the insight and the faith to obey the rubrics.

Thomas J. Talley

WHEN the patient is an adult recently reconverted to the Enemy's party, like your man, this is best done by encouraging him to remember, or to think he remembers, the parrotlike nature of his prayers in childhood. In reaction against that, he may be persuaded to aim at something entirely spontaneous, inward, informal, and unregularised; and what this will actually mean to a beginner will be an effort to produce in himself a vaguely devotional *mood* in which real concentration of will and intelligence have no part. One of their poets, Coleridge, has recorded that he did not pray "with moving lips and bended knees," but merely "composed his spirit to love" and indulged "a sense of supplication." That is exactly the sort of prayer we want; and since it bears a superficial resemblance to the prayer of silence as practised by those who are very far advanced in the Enemy's service, clever and lazy patients can be taken in by it for quite a long time. At the very least, they can be persuaded that the bodily position makes no difference to their prayers; for they constantly forget, what you must always remember, that they are animals and that whatever their bodies do affects their souls.

C. S. Lewis

FATHER, why does the church have so many vestments and ceremonies?" James asked his Pastor. "They're nice, but awfully out of date."

The priest smilingly replied: "Yes, James, but they do get you thinking on God in the right way and get you and those around you to do things worthwhile for heaven."

"You're right, Father, they keep your eyes, ears, hands, feet and even your knees pretty busy."

"And, James, notice how they raise your thoughts and heart to God, now in joy—again in sorrow. The church certainly knows what she is doing when she keeps all these sacred things. She alone can change them."

"Just like a game, Father," exclaimed James, "a lot of rules!"

"Yes, my boy, it reminds me of the game 'Follow the Leader.' But instead of calling it a game, the church calls it: 'The Liturgy.' Through the liturgy, the church whose head is Christ, glorifies God and draws men to God. It leads us daily in following Christ's life on earth. Pope Pius XII has said that by the liturgy *'the work of our redemption is continued and its fruits are applied to us.'* "

Baltimore Catechism

O BEDIENCE is a dance learned one step at a time, with faltering step perhaps. The pace may be halting; it is unfamiliar and we are clumsy. Our souls and hearts will be stretched. There will be pain—ask any dancer. But the stretching will leave our souls and hearts with a new breadth, and encompassed in the arms of our Lover God, we will know the freedom of the dance.

Cynthia Stebbins

A NY theory of ritual must recognize that, however factitive, efficacious and socially necessary the performance of certain rituals may be, their manner of work is different from that of ordinary labor and from (what shall we call it?) secular technique. As the Mbuti said of the *molimo*, "It was all dance, it was all song, it was all work, and it was all play."

The "showing forth" that belongs to ritual lifts it into an orbit of play, in which imagination runs ahead of visible, tangible reality, and things that may be, and might be, and ought or ought not to be, are given permission to happen in the playtime, of the ritual occasion. Rituals characteristically perform very serious and important work; but it is work done playfully, with that marveling combination of serious pretense and pretended seriousness that belongs to children and is revived in adults in the ritual mode of performance.

Tom F. Driver

THE justice of God presented in the liturgy is anything but an abstraction, for the liturgy of the church sacramentalizes the presence of Christ, the Just One. For that reason, and for that reason alone, we can say that the liturgy not only proclaims the justice of the kingdom of God as something to be done but actually renders it present, not as an achievement of ours but as a gift of God. In its presence we are confronted with that which we are called to be, with that which God would make us be, if we permit it. Thus the liturgy not only provides us with a moral ideal but confronts us with an ontological reality in the light of which the ambivalence of our own lives is revealed for what it is.

Like the word of God in history, the liturgy is the revelation of God's justice in both event and word, cutting into human life both as good news and as denunciation. It proclaims and realizes the saving presence of the Spirit in the world, brings the presence of the kingdom, and enables us to realize where this is happening even outside the liturgy. Celebrating the liturgy should train us to recognize justice and injustice when we see it. It serves as a basis for social criticism by giving us a criterion by which to evaluate the events and structures of the world. But it is not just the world "out there" that stands under the judgment of God's justice, sacramentally realized in the liturgy. The first accused is the church itself, which, to the degree that it fails to recognize what it is about, eats and drinks condemnation to itself (1 Corinthian 11:29).

In saying "Amen" to the justice of God proclaimed in the liturgy, we are implicitly saying "Anathema" to all that fails to measure up to that justice.

Mark Searle

THE world is
not with us enough.
O taste and see

the subway Bible poster said,
meaning The Lord, meaning
if anything all that lives
to the imagination's tongue,

grief, mercy, language,
tangerine, weather, to
breathe them, bite,
savor, chew, swallow, transform

into our flesh our
deaths, crossing the street, plum, quince,
living in the orchard and being

hungry, and plucking
the fruit.   Denise Levertov

IN the biblical story of creation the human being is presented, first of all, as a hungry being, and the whole world
as food. Second only to the direction to propagate and have
dominion over the earth, according to the author of the first
chapter of Genesis, is God's instruction to eat of the earth:
"Behold I have given you every herb bearing seed . . . and
every tree, which is the fruit of a tree yielding seed; to you
it shall be for meat." We must eat in order to live: We must
take the world into our body and transform it into ourselves,
into flesh and blood. We are indeed that which we eat, and
the whole world is presented as one all-embracing banquet
table. And this image of the banquet remains, throughout the
whole Bible, the central image of life. It is the image of life at
its creation and also the image of life at its end and fulfillment: Alexander
" . . . that you eat and drink at my table in my kingdom."   Schmemann

THE fruitful use of the liturgy then can be summed up in this experience of the mystery of Christ. Liturgical prayer does not endeavor to raise us up to something we are not: It reminds us that we have already been to some extent transformed; it assures us that the beginnings of transformation are a pledge and foreshadowing of its completion. The spiritual understanding of the psalter will therefore not introduce us to some esoteric technique of prayer, nor will it tempt us to induce within our minds some peculiar psychological state. It will, above all, tell us not merely what we ought to be but the unbelievable thing that we already *are.* It will tell us over and over again that we are Christ in this world, and that he lives in us, and that what was said of him has been and is being fulfilled in us; and that the last, most perfect fulfillment of all is now, at this moment, by the theological virtue of hope, placed in our hands. Thus the liturgy of earth is necessarily one with the liturgy of heaven. We are at the same time in the desert and in the promised land. The psalms are our bread of heaven in the wilderness of our exodus.

Thomas Merton

WE can interrupt here for a while this theme of food. We began with it only in order to free the terms "sacramental" and "eucharistic" from the connotations they have acquired in the long history of technical theology, where they are applied almost exclusively within the framework of "natural" *versus* "supernatural," and "sacred" *versus* "profane," that is, within the same opposition between religion and life which makes life ultimately unredeemable and religiously meaningless. In our perspective, however, the "original" sin is not primarily that humanity "disobeyed" God; the sin is that we ceased to be hungry for God and for God alone, ceased to see our whole life depending on the whole world as a sacrament of communion with God. The sin was not that we neglected religious duties. The sin was that we thought of God in terms of religion, i.e., opposing God to life. The only real fall is our noneucharistic life in a noneucharistic world. The fall is not that we preferred world to God, distorted the balance between the spiritual and material, but that we made the world *material,* whereas we were to have transformed it into the "life in God" filled with meaning and spirit.

Alexander
Schmemann

B EFORE we can begin to understand the symbolism of the eucharist or try to fathom the message it conveys, we need to remember hunger. Perhaps the older discipline in which the Catholic church imposed certain fasts on its adult members should have been adjusted to modern conditions rather than simply be allowed to be set aside without much thought. It is very important to remember hunger, and the fundamental way to know what hunger means is to be hungry. To understand very well what it means is to be very hungry over a long period of time. To understand in starkly revelatory depth what hunger means is to be starving, or to have developed authentic bridges of empathy to the experience of the starving.

Monica Hellwig

A ND I shall clothe myself in your eternal will, and by this light I shall come to know
that you, eternal Trinity,
are table
and food
and waiter for us.
You, eternal Father,
are the table
that offers us as food
the Lamb, your only-begotten Son.
He is the most exquisite of foods for us,
both in his teaching,
which nourishes us in your will,

and in the sacrament
that we receive in holy communion,
which feeds and strengthens us
while we are pilgrim travelers in this life.
And the Holy Spirit
is indeed a waiter for us,
for the Spirit serves us this teaching
by enlightening our mind's eye with it
and inspiring us to follow it.
And the Spirit serves us charity for our neighbors
and hunger to have as our food.

Catherine of Siena
Fourteenth century

N EAR the end of their peace pastoral, the U. S. bishops in
1982 urged the faithful to pray and fast for nuclear dis-
armament because of the danger the arms race poses. If they
were truly formed in the liturgy, several liturgists have argued,
they would have begun the pastoral with the argument,
"Because we are a people who pray and fast, we cannot
condone the nuclear arms race," and proceeded from there.

Robert McClory

E LECTED Silence, sing to me
And beat upon my whorlèd ear,
Pipe me to pastures still and be
The music that I care to hear.

Shape nothing, lips; be lovely-dumb:
It is the shut, the curfew sent
From there where all surrenders come
Which only makes you eloquent.

Be shellèd, eyes, with double dark
And find the uncreated light:
This ruck and reel which you remark
Coils, keeps, and teases simple sight.

Palate, the hutch of tasty lust,
Desire not to be rinsed with wine:
The can must be so sweet, the crust
So fresh that comes in fasts divine!

Nostrils, your careless breath that spend
Upon the stir and keep of pride,
What relish shall the censers send
Along the sanctuary side!

O feel-of-primrose hands, O feet
That want the yield of plushy sward,
But you shall walk the golden street
And you unhouse and house the Lord.

And, Poverty, be thou the bride
And now the marriage feast begun,
And lily-coloured clothes provide
Your spouse not laboured-at nor spun.

Gerard Manley
Hopkins
Nineteenth century

REJOICING, the church invokes Christ, having prepared a banquet, which seems worthy of heavenly feasting. And so the church says: "Let my beloved come into the garden and eat the fruits of the apple trees." What are these apple trees? You were made dry wood in Adam, but now through the grace of Christ you flower as apple trees.

Gladly did the Lord Jesus receive and with heavenly dignity reply to the church. He says: "I am come into my garden, I have gathered my myrrh with my aromatical spices, I have eaten my bread with my honey, I have drunk my wine with my milk." "Eat," he says, "my brothers and sisters, and be inebriated."

"I have gathered my myrrh with my aromatical spices."
What is this gathering? Recognize the vineyard, and you will
recognize the gathering. He says: "Thou hast brought a vineyard, out of Egypt," that is, the people of God. You are the
vineyard, you are the gathering, planted, as it were, as a vineyard, you are the gathering, who have yielded fruit.

Ambrose
Fourth century

Y*OU are drunk, but not with wine.*
    Isaiah 51:21

O God of too much giving, whence is this
inebriation that possesses me,
that the staid road now wanders all amiss
and that the wind walks much too giddily,
clutching a bush for balance, or a tree?
How then can dignity and pride endure
with such inordinate mirth upon the land,
when steps and speech are somewhat insecure
and the light heart is wholly out of hand?

If there be indecorum in my songs,
fasten the blame where rightly it belongs:
on him who offered me too many cups
of his most potent goodness—not on me,
a peasant who, because a King was host,
drank out of courtesy.

Jessica Powers

I F, then, you wish to understand the body of Christ, listen to
the apostle as he says to the faithful, "You are the body of
Christ, and his members" (1 Corinthians 12:27). If, therefore,
you are the body of Christ and his members, your mystery
has been placed on the Lord's table, you receive your mystery. You reply "Amen" to that which you are, and by reply-
ing you consent. For you hear "The body of Christ," and you
reply "Amen." Be a member of the body of Christ so that
your "Amen" may be true.

Augustine
Fifth century

CERTAINTY of the elect coming to be church
their pale clothes lavender the morning light
see where the bishop stands at the housedoor
brave in persecution ready to answer emperors
with the enlightened edge of his tongue

from the mountains they come down chewing mint
making their mouths pure for the celebration
of this most common food that understands them
into ecstasy, to eat the body of which they are the soul   Robert Kelly

WHAT is most striking about the traditional eucharistic elements of bread and wine is that neither are found in nature; rather, both are produce which requires a transformation of nature. Berries and spring water do not provide us with the elements of eucharist which requires gift of the earth, fruit of the vine *and work of human hands*. The co-operation between nature and humanity is implicit in the very elements of bread and wine. Furthermore, this co–operative venture presumes a long and reciprocal relationship. Bread is not produced overnight. The land needs to be cleared, seeds planted, crops tended, grain harvested, milled and baked. Then the land rests before the cycle begins again. And while a grain crop can be produced in a matter of a few months, the reciprocal relationship required of producing wine is even greater. Vines must be planted, tended and pruned for years before they produce a grape of any quality. Even after the harvesting of the grape, the produce needs to ferment and mature before achieving the dignity of wine. Thus, the very elements of bread and wine presume a symbiotic relationship between humankind and nature, especially for the sustained production of these elements.

Edward Foley,
Kathleen Hughes,
Gilbert Ostdiek

When Christians employed table bread and table wine for eucharist, the ritual implicitly acknowledged the need for people to cooperate with nature and with God. It was this tripartite relationship that enabled grain and grapes to be grown, bread and wine to be produced.

W E are the body of Christ"—that living bread which delights our eyes and noses, fingers and tongues with its sweetness and variety. Delicate little white dinner rolls, crusty wholemeal cobs, heavy rye sourdough, baps, stotties, cottages, croissants—we are all there in any Sunday congregation. Looking too good to eat, we have come nevertheless to be snapped, torn, passed in pieces from hand to hand, to be bitten, savored, chewed and swallowed. To dwell in the belly of our neighbors in Christ, to pass into their tissues and sustain their life.

The richness you spread before us in your body reminds us of those great feasts in which your stories body forth the mighty promise of God. And yet, dear Christ, you come to us as tiny fragments, a wafer, a token nibble of the loaf; not even a mouthful, let alone a meal. Bread of affliction you offer us, starvation rations with a little desert dust in it. As you promised we find that it sustains us, we are no longer hungry. But we have not had enough. We trudge on through the wilderness, singing praises to you for this manna, holding out our invitations to the wedding feast.

But this is it! This is the wedding feast where your fullness and your desolation join hands and will not be parted, here in this bread which we break in your name, and this cup that you dare us to drink.

Janet Gaden

W HEN I nourish myself, I am always eating a being which I have killed or which I have at least prevented from living. I eat an animal which has been killed for me, my life being preferred to its life. I eat something which would have engendered life or sustained the life of another living being: the egg which contained a life in germ, milk (and its derivatives) which were meant to assure the growth of a young animal, vegetables and fruit, the grain of wheat which was a seed. Thus to insure my life and my survival I must take or threaten the life of another being. I must induce death. I nourish myself with a life sacrificed for me.

In every act of nourishment there is therefore presence of life and death, a struggle for life against the danger of death, theft or gift of a life sacrificed in order to permit another to have life and to have it abundantly. The application of this to the eucharist is evident: In receiving the consecrated bread and wine I nourish myself with the life of the wheat and the grapes sacrificed for me but also with the body of Christ given for me and with his blood shed for me. . . .

Every morsel of bread is the product and the result of an entire history. First, in the season for planting the grains of wheat are thrown into the bosom of the earth, which is a fertile mother, and after an apparent death and time of gestation or germination, we, marveling, see a blade grow. Thus the symbolism of bread implies in the first place the image of death and resurrection in the bosom of the earth, and it is understandable that in several mystery cults the history of the grain of wheat was considered a symbol of human history. Subsequently the grain, carefully harvested, is crushed, ground, almost annihilated; countless grains are pulverized and mingled to make flour, which, thanks to human work and the action of fire, finally becomes bread. . . .

Bread is much more than an element of nourishment: It is a symbol of work and a symbol of life and, when shared, it is charged with familial and social values.

Like bread, wine is the product of a long and careful preparation. Before tasting wine we must plant the vine, prune it, harvest the grapes, put them under the press, much as we ground the wheat grain, let the juice ferment, and finally age the wine. Wine is made by human beings, exclusively for human use.

Wine gives vigor and vitality. Because of its red color, and because it springs forth from the cluster of grapes, it is often associated with blood, and this association was adopted by Christ in the eucharist. Wine is regarded as a beverage of life and immortality. . . .

Wine is furthermore an efficacious symbol of sharing and communion. Members of a group gathered to celebrate together drink from the same cup, or at least they toast each other, signifying with that gesture their intention of drinking symbolically from one cup. . . .

The bread and wine are complementary. The two respond to two essential urges of the human animal, the bread to our hunger, and the wine to our thirst. The bread is the fruit of the earth, a fertile mother, while the wine appears more as the fruit of the sun, without which nothing grows. Bread is a material food which insures existence, while wine is a spiritual beverage which incites to action and to the transcending of the daily limits of existence. The bread is assimilated and transformed in our body, while the wine has the power to transform us to cause us to become other.

Philippe Rouillard

As practiced in a variety of religions, a meal has certainly acquired many cultic connotations as sacrifice and godly feast, but the eating and drinking that are the heart of the Christian eucharist are modest and sober, taking their meaning from domestic meals rather than from cultic meals. Indeed, the New Testament literature does not use cultic language for the church's acts of worship, but transfers this kind of language to the people themselves or to the death of Christ. It is in holiness, obedience, and willing testimony to God's love, and in the hope rooted in this, that all worship is fulfilled and thus changed radically. The eucharist is a celebration and an act of worship because of the people who celebrate it in faith. If those participating do not live the gospel fellowship in earnest, their act is more a profanation than a proclamation of the Lord's death.

David N. Power

We have just heard in the gospel that those who surrender to the service of people through love of Christ will live like the grain of wheat that dies. This hope comforts us as Christians. We know that every effort to improve society, above all when society is so full of injustice and sin, is an effort that God blesses, wants and demands. We have the security of knowing that what we plant, if nourished with Christian hope, will never fail.

This holy Mass, this eucharist, is clearly an act of faith. This body broken and blood shed for human beings encourages us to give our body and blood up to suffering and pain, as Christ did—not for self, but to bring justice and peace to our people. Let us be intimately united in faith and hope at this moment.

At this point, Archbishop Romero was shot to death.   Oscar Romero

A T the heart of it all is the eucharistic action, a thing of an absolute simplicity—the taking, blessing, breaking and giving of bread and the taking, blessing and giving of a cup of wine and water, as these were first done with their new meaning by a young Jew before and after supper with his friends on the night before he died. Soon it was simplified still further, by leaving out the supper and combining the double grouping before and after it into a single rite. So the four-action shape of the liturgy was found by the end of the first century. He had told his friends to do this henceforward with the new meaning "for the *anamnesis*" of him, and they have done it always since.

Was ever another command so obeyed? For century after century, spreading slowly to every continent and country and among every race on earth, this action has been done, in every conceivable human circumstance, for every conceivable human need from infancy and before it to extreme old age and after it, from the pinnacles of earthly greatness to the refuge of fugitives in the caves and dens of the earth. We have found no better thing than this to do for kings at their crowning and for criminals going to the scaffold; for armies in triumph or for a bride and bridegroom in a little country church; for the proclamation of a dogma or for a good crop of wheat; for the wisdom of the Parliament of a mighty nation or for a sick old woman afraid to die; for a schoolboy sitting an examination or for Columbus setting out to discover America; for the famine of whole provinces or for the soul of a dead lover; in thankfulness because my father did not die of pneumonia; for a village headman much tempted to return to fetish because the yams have failed; because the Turk was at the gates of Vienna; for the repentance of Margaret; for the settlement of a strike; for a son for a barren woman; for Captain so-and-so, wounded and prisoner of war; while the lions roared in the nearby amphitheater; on the beach at Dunkirk; while the hiss of scythes in the thick June grass came faintly through the windows of the church; tremulously, by an old monk on the fiftieth anniversary of his vows; furtively, by an exiled bishop who had hewn timber all day in a prison camp near Murmansk; gorgeously, for the canonization of St. Joan of Arc—one could fill many pages with the reasons why we have done this, and not tell a hundredth part of them. And best of all, week by week and month by month, on a hundred thousand successive Sundays, faithfully, unfailingly, across all the parishes of Christendom, the pastors have done this just to *make* the *plebs sancta Dei*—the holy common people of God.

To those who know a little of Christian history probably the most moving of all the reflections it brings is not the thought of the great events and the well-remembered saints, but of those innumerable millions of entirely obscure faithful men and women, every one with his or her own individual hopes and fears and joys and sorrows and loves—and sins and temptations and prayers—once every whit as vivid and alive as mine are now. They have left no slightest trace in this world, not even a name, but have passed to God utterly forgotten by us. Yet each of them once believed and prayed as I believe and pray, and found it hard and grew slack and sinned and repented and fell again. Each of them worshiped at the eucharist, and found their thoughts wandering and tried again, and felt heavy and unresponsive and yet knew —just as really and pathetically as I do these things. There is a little ill-spelled ill-carved rustic epitaph of the fourth century from Asia Minor: "Here sleeps the blessed Chione, who has found Jerusalem for she prayed much." Not another word is know of Chione, some peasant woman who lived in that vanished world of Christian Anatolia. But how lovely if all that should survive after sixteen centuries were that one had prayed much, so that the neighbors who saw all one's life were sure one must have found Jerusalem! What did the Sunday eucharist in her village church every week for a lifetime mean to the blessed Chione—and to the millions like her then, and every year since? The sheer stupendous quantity of the love of God which this ever repeated action has drawn from the obscure Christian multitude through the centuries is in itself an overwhelming thought.   Gregory Dix

NOW about the eucharist: This is how to give thanks. First in connection with the cup: "We thank you, our Father, for the holy vine of David, your child, which you have revealed through Jesus, your child. To you be glory forever."

Then in connection with the piece [broken off the loaf]: "We thank you, our Father, for the life and knowledge which you have revealed through Jesus, your child. To you be glory forever. As this piece [of bread] was scattered over the hills and then was brought together and made one, so let your church be brought together from the ends of the earth into your kingdom. For yours is the glory and the power through Jesus Christ forever."

You must not let anyone eat or drink of your eucharist except those baptized in the Lord's name. For in reference to this the Lord said, "Do not give what is sacred to dogs."

After you have finished your meal, say grace in this way: "We thank you, holy Father, for your sacred name which you have lodged in our hearts, and for the knowledge and faith and immortality which you have revealed through Jesus, your child. To you be glory forever. Almighty Master, you have created everything for the sake of your name, and have given all people food and drink to enjoy that they may thank you. But to us you have given spiritual food and drink and eternal life through Jesus, your child. Above all, we thank you that you are mighty. To you be glory forever.

"Remember, Lord, your church, to save it from all evil and to make it perfect by your love. Make it holy, and gather it together from the four winds into your kingdom which you have made ready for it. For yours is the power and the glory forever."

Didache
Second century

THOSE who have more come to the aid of those who lack, and we are constantly together. Over all that we receive we bless the Maker of all things through his Son Jesus Christ and through the Holy Spirit. And on the day called Sunday there is a meeting in one place of those who live in cities or the country, and the memoirs òf the apostles or the writing of the prophets are read as long as time permits. Then we all stand up together and offer prayers. And, as said before, when we have finished the prayer, bread is brought, and wine and water, and the president similarly sends up prayers and thanksgivings to the best of his ability, and the congregation assents, saying the Amen; the distribution and reception of the consecrated [elements] by each one takes place and they are sent to the absent by the deacons. Those who prosper, and who so wish, contribute, each one as much as each chooses to. What is collected is deposited with the president, and he takes care of orphans and widows, and those who are in want on account of sickness or any other cause, and those who are in bonds, and the strangers who are sojourners among [us], and, briefly, he is the protector of all those in need. We all hold this common gathering on Sunday, since it is the first day, on which God transforming darkness and matter made the universe, and Jesus Christ our Savior rose from the dead on the same day.

Justin
Second century

AFTER the people have presented their gifts, the archdeacon, at a signal from the pope, goes to the altar and, with the help of a subdeacon, arranges the breads that are to be consecrated. The chalice is placed on the altar and water is added to the wine by one of the members of the singing choir. After all this is done the pontiff leaves his place and kisses the altar and then himself receives the oblation of the assisting clerics. Lastly he lays his own oblation (two small loaves brought for this purpose from the Lateran) on the altar. . . .

Then begins the canon, taking the word in the comprehensive meaning it then had. Each one has taken an appointed place. Normally that would mean that the pope, coming from his *cathedra,* would stand behind the altar facing the people. . . .

The pope begins the prayer in a loud voice. The subdeacons respond to the introductory versicles and take up the singing of the *Sanctus.* The pope alone stands once more erect and continues the prayer, while the others remain bowed. The words of consecration, like all the other parts of the canon are said audibly; otherwise there is nothing distinctive about them. . . . When the pope elevates the host in the sight of all and recites the final doxology, it is the archdeacon's duty to take the chalice by the handles—holding it with a cloth called the *offertorium*—and to lift it, too, on high. The canon is therefore quite simple and free of any other display. The "action," as it is termed, simply presents the pontiff's sacramental word, with no ornament other than his prayers.

Joseph Jungmann

I used to look forward to evening Mass in Ole Sikii's village. It began when I drove my Landrover up to his village. The cows were just returning with their tired and parched herders. Children swarmed all over me with their heads bowed low in the typical gesture of a young Masai person greeting an adult. They waited to be touched on the top of the head, and if you did not do it, they kept butting you gently until you did. Elders left their work of standing at the various gates, supervising the return of the cows, assuring themselves that each cow, by name not by number, had returned safely, greeted me and went back to their work. Mothers, scattered throughout the village near all their houses, had already began the milking of the returning cows, but they heard you come in.

In every house in the village, the consciousness of the evening Mass had penetrated to some extent. In varying degrees, everyone in the village was thinking of the Mass, was turning towards the Mass, in a sense was already participating in the Mass, because it began when I drove in. Or long before. It was a strange kind of Mass. No church building, not even any special, fixed spot where it took place. As a matter of fact it moved around all over the village. It started in the spot where several elders had lighted a fire from two sticks of wood, even before I arrived.

An important act, on my part, before I entered the village, was to stoop down, scoop up a handful of grass, and present it to the first elders who greeted me. Grass was another sacred sign among the Masai, like spittle. Since their cattle, and they themselves, lived off grass, it was a vital and holy sign to them, a sign of peace and happiness and well-being.

During stormy and angry arguments that might arise in their lives, a tuft of grass, offered by one Masai and accepted by the second, was an assurance that no violence would erupt because of the differences and arguments. No Masai would violate that sacred sign of peace offered, because it was not only a sign of peace; it *was* peace. Just as spittle was forgiveness. Such was the sacramental system of the Masai.

So, as the Mass began, I picked up a tuft of grass and passed it on to the first elder who met me, and greeted him with "the peace of Christ." He accepted it and passed it on to his family, and they passed it on to neighboring elders and their families. It had to pass all through the village.

The Mass moved from the place of the fire lighting to the place of the passing of the grass to the dancing area where dancing was always done in the village. The singing began not long after I got there, and that singing was not choir practice. It was the Mass. I never told these people which songs to sing. They sang what they wanted to sing and when they wanted to. Ole Sikii's community was the first to enshrine Christian thoughts in Masai music.

The dancers of another tribe, which began to be evangelized shortly after the Masai tribe, did a very interesting thing during the Mass in their area. This was the Sonjo tribe and they were very expert dancers. They brought their music directly to the place where the bread and wine were later to be blessed, and performed it there deliberately and carefully. Some of their music was decidedly secular. The elders in that community pointed out to me that the purpose of such a procedure was to make an actual judgment on a very important area of their lives. The time of the eucharist was the time for that judgment. They were not ashamed of that particular dance in their own lives, so they wanted that part of their lives to be offered with the eucharist. There were some dances they were ashamed to bring into the eucharist. By that very fact, a judgment had been made on them. Such dances should no longer be a part of their lives at all. Eucharist served as a judgment for them.   Vincent Donovan

O UR surrender to God through the Word-made-flesh and in the Spirit is what enables the new birth to happen and the new person to emerge. Freedom and solidarity are the new characteristics. Whatever terms we use for them, the profound realities of liberation and of human unity adequately describe the meaning of redemption and salvation. The one God frees us from all our other gods. The one God joins us all as sisters and as brothers, loved so that we can be loving.

All of Christian liturgy (and preeminently the Sunday eucharist, where the church is built up, actualized both as local assembly and in relation to the other churches) is an acting out of the freedom and solidarity in God, "playing kingdom," as it has been called. It is not merely one of the activities of the church. It is the key and critical ecclesial moment. It is a going apart from the world for the sake of serving the world. It is an experience of the reign of God, where all are free and all are one, for the sake of the earth, where we are all in different stages and conditions of unfreedom and division.

"Your will be done on earth as in heaven" is part of the most familiar refrain of Christian prayer. If one were to express surprise every time the sun rises in the morning, if the daily repetition of nature's course provoked the same question day after day (what is the connection between morning and the appearance of the sun?), it would be no more strange than it is for Christians to exhibit a naive wonder (if nothing worse) every time they confront an intimation that Christian discipleship requires a common (church) effort to change the political-economic-cultural conditions of human life and society.

This means that Christian faith essentially involves an effort to bring the reign of God to bear on the status quo. This means that if I am comfortable with the way things are in the world and don't want anything to be disturbed, I am not a viable candidate for baptism or eucharist. This means that there is a helluva tension between the kind of life the Christian believes that God wills for the human family and the kind of life we earth people have thus far achieved.

Robert W. Hovda

A word has to be said regarding that widely held view of life and especially liturgy as a play, as a cosmic play with passion and earnestness but without the ultimately tragic, with rules to be followed but only for the "time-being." Liturgy is the re-enactment of the total world-play on a human scale. Life enters into the forms of worship, because worship does not claim anything else than to be the very quintessence of human life, expressing not only its individual symbolism but also its cosmic destiny and vocation.

Raimondo Panikkar

EXPLOITATION and rejection, suffering and death, failure to show a clear path to identity and self-worth are as much a part of the cultural experience of our children as belonging and sharing and nurturance and affirmation. The focus on the latter and the denial of the former must result in a distortion of the message of salvation.

Mary Collins

Persons of intelligence, good will, and religious sensibility can claim that electronically amplified renditions of the world have no effect and are thus no problem. Such a claim denies the problem that when those who have been soaking up TV fare cross the threshold into the sacred space where the community gathers, they cross with that fare as part of their lives, if not in their actual mindset then at least in their memories.

Michael Warren

The Christian liturgy has never hesitated to speak, *simultaneously,* a language of sin and a language of healing. . . . The simultaneous presence of both languages creates a tension that makes festivity possible. For unless festivity can deal with the unavoidable ambiguity of real life—its scabs and its successes—it becomes escapist. By insisting that we acknowledge our pain—our failure and our finitude—the festivity of worship offers us the possibility of moving *beyond* it toward a vision of humanity healed and reconciled.

Nathan Mitchell

Our problem is how to live what we pray, how to make our lives a daily commentary on our prayer book, how to live in consonance with what we promise, how to keep faith with the vision we pronounce.

Abraham Joshua Heschel

But anyway I like parts of my prayers to stay the same and part to change. So many prayer books are so awful, but if you stick with the liturgy, you are safe.

Flannery O'Connor

W HEN the guru sat down to worship each evening the ashram cat would get in the way and distract the worshipers. So he ordered that the cat be tied during evening worship.

After the guru died the cat continued to be tied during evening worship. And when the cat expired, another cat was brought to the ashram so that it could be duly tied during evening worship.

Centuries later learned treatises were written by the guru's scholarly disciples on the liturgical significance to tying up a cat while worship is performed.

Anthony de Mello

A DDRESSING God in faith and praise is a matter of doing so from within the memory of the event and in the midst of the experience whence the holy comes. Such naming invites us to transcend our own idealized view of the holy, to accept God's coming in tragedy, in the poor and the lowly, in the humanly marginal, in humanity's community with earth, yea even among the dead. The naming of liturgy, like the naming of biblical revelation, is a transfer of names that disorients and uproots in order to redescribe and reorient. As the Almighty was named for the nomadic tribes of the exodus, or for the people of the kingdom brought into captivity, for the lowly maiden of Nazareth, or for the disciples of the crucified, so God continues to be named for those who perished in the Holocaust and for those who survived the Holocaust, for those who fell victim to the nation's failure in Vietnam and for those who survived it, for the slaves who furnished the labor for a new democratic nation and for those who now know the weakness of building on the exploited, for the women who survived by Sophia and for those born of these women, for the earth exploited by human audacity and for those who lament it. The Blessed One is the one blessed by the sick and the suffering, by the liminal and the forgotten, and by the compassionate who are not fearful of the invitation into such circles. We do not need so much to find new names as to know where to utter them and to what to relate them. The sacred circle has a tremendous power to reveal for those who dance.

David N. Power

W̲E are what we repeatedly do. Excellence then is not an act, but a habit.

Aristotle
Fourth century BCE

T̲HOSE who plead for the primacy of the prayer of expression over the prayer of empathy ought to remember that the ability to express what is hidden in the heart is a rare gift, and cannot be counted upon by all. What, as a rule, makes it possible for us to pray is our ability to affiliate our own minds with the pattern of fixed texts, to unlock our hearts to the words, and to surrender to their meanings. The words stand before us as living entities full of spiritual power, of a power which often surpasses the grasp of our minds. The words are often the givers, and we the recipients. They inspire our minds and awaken our hearts.

It is good that there are words sanctified by ages of worship, by the honesty and love of generations. If it were left to ourselves, who would know what word is right to be offered as praise in the sight of God or which of our perishable thoughts is worthy of entering eternity?

On the other hand, one may ask: Why should we follow the order of the liturgy? Should we not say, one ought to pray when one is ready to pray? The time to pray is all the time. There is always an opportunity to disclose the holy, but when we fail to seize it, there are definite moments in the liturgical order of the day, there are words in the liturgical order of our speech to remind us. These words are like mountain peaks pointing to the unfathomable. Ascending their trails we arrive at prayer.

Abraham Joshua
Heschel

A̲FTER many years of vain attempts to "explain" God as trinity, I now say, "Well, to begin with we Christians have been taught to pray, 'Our Father, who art in heaven . . .'" I then suggest that a good place to begin to understand what we Christians are about is to join me in that prayer.

For to learn to pray is no easy matter but requires much training, not unlike learning to lay brick. It does no one any good to believe in God, at least the God we find in Jesus of Nazareth, if they have not learned to pray. To learn to pray means we must acquire humility not as something we try to do, but as commensurate with the practice of prayer. In short, we do not believe in God, become humble, and then learn to pray, but in learning to pray we humbly discover we cannot do other than believe in God.

But, of course, to learn to pray requires we learn to pray with other Christians. It means we must learn the disciplines necessary to worship God. Worship, at least for Christians, is the activity to which all our skills are ordered. That is why there can be no separation of Christian morality from Christian worship. As Christians, our worship is our morality, for it is in worship we find ourselves engrafted into the story of God. It is in worship that we acquire the skills to acknowledge who we are—sinners.

Stanley Hauerwas

"FULL, active, and conscious" participation in the liturgy depends . . . first . . . upon our acquaintance with prayer in daily life—over the whole range of our community. . . .

Liturgy is the on-going mutuality of God and our humanity. The liturgy exists to glorify God and to proclaim the mystery of faith while sanctifying all that is human before God. In this sense glorifying God, giving praise and thanks together, is a way of coming to know the divine life. Yet this is precisely how my life comes to fullest truth and to the realization of what it is to exist in faith: to discover and to welcome the gift of creatureliness and to perceive holiness in all times and places. This means that even the cry of pain and the remembrance of suffering and complexity may commingle with the praise and thanks. These are offered together in solidarity with the whole church. My daily life is not fully received until it is joined with others in praise of God.

T. S. Eliot expressed this well in "Choruses from 'The Rock'":
What life have you if you have not life together?
There is no life that is not in community,
And no community not lived in praise of God.   Don E. Saliers

FOR Christians the beginning of the day should not be burdened and oppressed with besetting concerns for the day's work. At the threshold of the new day stands the Lord who made it. All the darkness and distraction of the dreams of night retreat before the clear light of Jesus Christ and his wakening word. All unrest, all impurity, all care and anxiety flee before him. Therefore, at the beginning of the day let all distraction and empty talk be silenced and let the first thought and the first word belong to him to whom our whole life belongs. "Sleeper awake! Rise from the dead, and Christ will shine on you" (Ephesians 5:14).

The household is united at the evening table and the last devotion. With the disciples in Emmaus they pray: "Abide with us: for it is toward evening, and the day is far spent" (Luke 24:29). It is an excellent thing if the evening devotion can be held at the actual end of the day, thus becoming the last word before the night's rest. When night falls, the true light of God's word shines brighter for the church. The prayer of the psalms, a hymn, and common prayer close the day, as they opened it.   Dietrich Bonhoeffer

THE cloud of cells awakens, intensifies, swarms . . . the cells dance inside beams of sunlight so thin we cannot see them. . . . To them each ray is a vast palace, with thousands of rooms. From the dance of the cells praise sentences rise to the throat of the man praying and singing alone in his room. He lets his arms climb above his head, and says, "Now do you still say you cannot choose the Road?"   Robert Bly

ACH day Christians pray that in and through the church the time of this world may become the new time for the children of light, may be filled with new light for those whom the church has brought to life. And so the church "refers" this day to that which constitutes its own life, to the reality of the Presence which the church alone in this world knows, and alone is able to reveal.

Alexander
Schmemann

WE bring to night prayer all that fell apart during the day. At bedside or in community, we tend to go down on our knees or to bow deeply, face to the ground: not only repenting it all but passing up the chance to defend ourselves. The words are acknowledgment that we have participated in the evil done and the good not done. But they are more than this. In our tradition, it is as if sleep is that altar which we may not approach unreconciled with God, with creation and one another.

The ground of that reconciliation is the mercy of God, implored and certainly expected—as are its reforming consequences. But really, there is little here about tomorrow (all of night prayer is a little doubtful about tomorrow, a little indifferent even). It is enough that before sleep we are reconciled. If there is a tomorrow, then at its end I will again ask for this mercy, again repent, again make my peace. Ours is a *habit* of reconciling. Stories from many cultures tell us that sleep and the conscience are somehow bound. Most of us recognize that most famous of sleepwalkers, Lady Macbeth, the first time we meet her.

All this is quite different from a reckoning. We are not about settling accounts—what I owe, what is owed to me—at bedside. It is more like playing out the parable of the laborers in the vineyard: Let God be good and hold no grudge; let us be as much in that mold of goodness as we can.

From such a habit, what can we say of peace? Something fundamental about ourselves. We are ready to say, "I confess." Ready because we do it daily. I confess. Even if I am

a poor person who today has inflicted no harm on the creation but have borne suffering, I speak as the church, saying:
I confess. It is not pleasant, but it is how we approach the
making of peace: It has to do with our hearts—the disarma-
ment of our defense and excuses, the posture of simplicity,
the recognition of our own simplicity in the sufferings of
the world.
Gabe Huck

O radiant Light, O Sun divine
  of God the Father's deathless face,
O Image of the light sublime
that fills the heavenly dwelling place,

O Son of God, the source of life,
praise is your due by night and day.
Our happy lips must raise the strain
of your esteemed and splendid name.

Lord Jesus Christ, as daylight fades,
as shine the lights of eventide,
we praise the Father with the Son,
the Spirit blest, and with them one.
Phos Hilaron
Third century

O splendor of God's glory bright,
  from light eternal bringing light;
thou light of life, light's living spring,
true day, all day illumining:

Come, Holy Sun of heavenly love,
shower down thy radiance from above,
and to our inward hearts convey
the Holy Spirit's cloudless ray.

O joyful be the passing day
with thoughts as clear as morning's ray,
with faith like noontide shining bright,
our souls unshadowed by the night.

O Lord, with each returning morn
thine image to our hearts is born;
O may we ever clearly see
our Savior and our God in thee!

Ambrose
Fourth century

ONE of the first things I noticed on my longer retreats, when I was with the monks in choir four or five times a day for a week or more, was how like an exercise class the liturgy seemed. It was sometimes difficult to rise early for morning office; at other times during the day it seemed tedious to be going back to church, but knowing that the others would be there made all the difference. Once there, the benefits were tangible, and I usually wondered how I could have wished to be anywhere else. When I compared all this to an aerobics class, a monk said, "That's exactly right."

But monastic fidelity to the liturgy is the antithesis of narcissism. It is serious play indeed. It means that somewhere, as I write this, as you read it, people are singing psalms and praying for us all. Knowing that most of us won't notice or care, they are making us a gift of their very lives. Here we approach the ultimate play in a monastery, the monk's sense that his being there at all is a sign of God's play with him. . . .

The monks will have recreation in the cloister; I'll walk the monastery grounds. Coyotes will begin calling in the coulees to the north. Soon, the monks, too, will begin to sing, the gentle lullaby of vespers and compline, at one with the rhythm of evening, the failing light and the rise of the moon. Together, monks and coyotes will sing the world to sleep.

Kathleen Norris

THE Visitor shuffled documents. Jocelin waited, hands clasped before his chest, as he inspected the row of sandals under the table. Presently the Visitor looked up.

"Would you agree that the, what is referred to here as 'The Rich Fabric of Constant Praise' has been unnecessarily interrupted?"

Jocelin nodded emphatically.

"It's true. How true it is! So true!"

"Explain then."

"Before we began to build, we sealed off the east end as best we could, and held the services in the Lady Chapel."

"It's the common practice."

"So at that time the services continued. But later, you see, men felt there was some danger. When the pillars began to sing, and then bend, there was none of the Chapter, none of the laity, no one who dared worship there."

"In fact, the services of the church came to an end?"

Jocelin looked up quickly and spread his hands.

"No. Not if you can see—all the complications. I was there, all the time. It was a kind of service. I was there, and they were there, adding glory to the house."

"They?"

"The workmen. There were fewer and fewer of them of course; but some stayed right to the end."

The Visitor said nothing; but he felt himself understood, and hurried on.

William Golding

CHRIST, mighty Savior, light of all creation,
you make the daytime radiant with the sunlight
And to the night give glittering adornment,
Stars in the heavens.

Now comes the day's end as the sun is setting,
Mirror of daybreak, pledge of resurrection;
While in the heavens choirs of stars appearing
Hallow the nightfall.

Therefore we come now, evening rites to offer,
Joyfully chanting holy hymns to praise you,
With all creation joining hearts and voices
Singing in your glory.

Give heed, we pray you, to our supplication:
That you may grant us pardon for offenses,
Strength for our weak hearts, rest for aching bodies,
Soothing the weary.

Though bodies slumber, hearts shall keep their vigil.
For ever resting in the peace of Jesus,
In light or darkness worshiping our Savior
Now and for ever.

Mozarabic Rite
Tenth century

WE read and reread these opening pages of Genesis, along with certain sequences of psalms, and recover these deep, elemental rhythms, internalizing the reality in which the strong, initial pulse is God's creating/saving word, God's providential/sustaining presence, God's grace.

As this biblical genesis rhythm works in me, I also discover something else: When I quit my day's work, nothing essential stops. I prepare for sleep not with a feeling of exhausted frustration because there is so much yet undone and unfinished, but with expectancy. The day is about to begin! God's genesis words are about to be spoken again. During the hours of my sleep, how will God prepare to use my obedience, service and speech when morning breaks? I go to sleep to get out of the way for awhile. I get into the rhythm of salvation. While we sleep, great and marvelous things, far beyond our capacities to invent or engineer, are in process— the moon marking the seasons, the lion roaring for its prey, the earthworms aerating the earth, the stars turning in their courses, the proteins repairing our muscles, our dreaming brains restoring a deeper sanity beneath the gossip and scheming of our waking hours. Our work settles into the context of God's work. Human effort is honored and respected not as a thing in itself but by its integration into the rhythms of grace and blessing.

Eugene H. Peterson

Prayer, the church's banquet, angels' age,
God's breath in man returning to his birth,
The soul in paraphrase, heart in pilgrimage,
The Christian plummet sounding heaven and earth;

Engine against th' Almighty, sinner's tower,
Reverséd thunder, Christ-side-piercing spear,
The six-days' world transposing in an hour,
A kind of tune, which all things hear and fear;

Softness, and peace, and joy, and love, and bliss,
Exalted manna, gladness of the best,
Heaven in ordinary, man well dressed,
The Milky Way, the bird of Paradise,

Church bells beyond the stars heard, the soul's blood,
The land of spices; something understood.

George Herbert
Seventeenth century

Strive to render your mind deaf and dumb during prayer: then you will be able to pray as you ought.

When you meet with temptation, or are irritated by someone's disagreement, so that you are filled with anger against the one who has disagreed with you, or even say some unseemly word, remember prayer and the judgment (of your conscience before the face of God) during it, and the unseemly movement will at once be stilled in you.

Anything you may do to revenge yourself upon a brother who has done you an injustice will offend you during prayer.

Prayer is a branch (of the tree) of meekness, and freedom from anger.

Prayer is an expression of joy and thankfulness.

Nilus of Sinai
Fifth century

Prayer is a remedy against sorrow and depression.

B EFORE all else, let us list sincere thanksgiving first on the scroll of our prayer. On the second line, we should put confession and heartfelt contrition of soul. Then let us present our petition to the King of all. This is the best way of prayer.

John Climacus
Seventh century

A FTER the maggid's death, his disciples came together and talked about the things he had done. When it was Rabbi Schneur Zalman's turn, he asked them: "Do you know why our master went to the pond every day at dawn and stayed there for a while before coming home again?" They did not know why. Rabbi Zalman continued: "He was learning the song with which the frogs praise God. It takes a very long time to learn that song."

Martin Buber

Y OU have first loved us, O God, alas. We speak of it in terms of history, as if you have only loved us first but a single time, rather than that without ceasing you have loved us first many times and every day and our whole life through. . . . If I rise at dawn and at the same time turn my soul towards you in prayers, you are there ahead of me; you have loved me first. When I withdraw from the distractions of the day and turn my soul in thought towards you, you are the first and thus forever. And yet we always speak ungratefully as if you have loved us first only once.

Soren Kierkegaard

APPLAUD,
little gods, applaud
your God,
you own your glory!
Bow low
when The Holy looms,
the voice
looms in from the sea,
God, God,
booming in thunder,
God, loose,
out, over the deep,
strong voice,
power itself, bright
voice, light
itself, loose from God,
splitting
cedars to splinters,
cedars
of Lebanon, God's sharp
blows are
licks of fire, down, down,
they bounce
the earth, bounce the hills
like beasts,
wild, skipping oxen.
Thunder!
God buckles the fields.
Thunder!
God labors the deer
and bares
the forests of leaves.
Thunder!
God's temple flares up,
flares with
visions of glory!

The throne
of God since chaos,
the throne
of God forever!
God, God,
maker of triumph,
God, God,
of chaos and peace!

Francis Patrick Sullivan
Psalm 29

Wʜᴀᴛ keeps us from sleeping
is that
they have threatened us with resurrection.

Accompany us, then,
on this vigil
and you will know
how marvelous it is
to live
threatened with resurrection.

Julia Esquivel

Wʜʏ is the number forty observed if not that the excellence of the Decalogue is perfected by the four books of the gospel? For as ten multiplied by four make forty, so we perfectly fulfill the precepts of the Decalogue when we faithfully observe the four books of the holy gospels. From this another thing may be learned. In this mortal body we are composed of four elements; and it is because of this same body we are made subject to God's commandments. The commands of the law are given to us in the Decalogue. And since it is through the desires of the body we have despised the commandments of the Decalogue, it is just that we chastize this same flesh four times ten times.

And if you wish there is yet another thing to be understood from this time of Lent. From this present day till the joyful solemnities of Easter there are six weeks; that is, two and forty days. From which if you subtract the six Sundays there remain six and thirty days of abstinence. And since a year continues throughout three hundred and sixty-five days, we, when we mortify ourselves for thirty-six days, give to the Lord a tithe as it were for our year; so that we who have lived for ourselves throughout the year we have received, may, during this tenth of it, die to our maker through abstinence.

Gregory the Great
Sixth century

To do justice to the mystery of Easter joy with the stale words of human speech is rather difficult. This is so not only because every mystery of the gospel penetrates only with difficulty into the narrow confines of human life—thereby making it even harder for our words to grasp and contain and express these mysteries—but because the Easter message is the most human tidings of Christianity. That is why we find it the most difficult message to understand. For what is most true, most obvious and most easy, is the most difficult to be, to do and to believe. That is to say, modern people base life on the unexpressed, and therefore all the more self-evident, prejudice that anything "religious" is merely an affair of the most interior heart and of the loftiest spirit—something that we must bring about by ourselves, something, therefore, that involves the difficulties and unreality of the heart's thoughts and moods.

But Easter tells us that God has done something. God has. And this action has not merely gently touched the heart of a person here and there, so that they tremble slightly from an ineffable and nameless someone. God has raised the Son from the dead. God has done this—has conquered—not merely in the realm of inwardness, in the realm of thought, but in the realm where we, the glory of the human mind notwithstanding, are most really ourselves: in the actuality of this world, far from all "mere" thoughts and "mere" sentiments. God has conquered in the realm where we experience practically what we are in essence: children of the earth, who die.

Karl Rahner

ON this day you shall explain to your son, "This is because of what the LORD did for me when I came out of Egypt." It shall be as a sign on your hand and as a reminder on your forehead; thus the law of the LORD will ever be on your lips, because with a strong hand the LORD brought you out of Egypt. Therefore, you shall keep this prescribed rite at its appointed time from year to year.

Exodus 13:8–10

THIS is the day on which the church celebrates the eucharist—the sacrament of its ascension to the kingdom and of its participation in the messianic banquet in the "age to come," the day on which the church fulfills itself as new life. The earliest documents mention that Christians meet *statu die*—on a fixed day—and nothing in the long history of Christianity could alter the importance of this fixed day.

A "fixed day." If Christianity were a purely "spiritual" and eschatological faith there would have been no need for a "fixed day," because mysticism has no interest in time. To save one's soul one needs, indeed, no "calendar." And if Christianity were but a new "religion," it would have established its calendar, with the usual opposition between the "holy days" and the "profane days"—those to be "kept" and "observed" and those religiously insignificant. Both understandings did in fact appear later. But this was not at all the original meaning of the "fixed day." It was not meant to be a "holy day" opposed to profane ones, a commemoration in time of a past event. Its true meaning was in the transformation of time, not of calendar. For, on the one hand, Sunday remained *one of the days* (for more than three centuries it was not even a day of rest), the first of the week, fully belonging to *this* world. Yet on the other hand, on that day, through the eucharistic ascension, the Day of the Lord was revealed and manifested in all its glory and transforming power as the *end* of this world, as the *beginning* of the world to come. And thus through that one day all days, all time, were transformed into times of *remembrance and expectation,* remembrance of this ascension, ("we have seen the true light") and expectation of its *coming.* All days, all hours were now referred to this *end* of all "natural" life, to the *beginning* of the new life. The week was no longer a sequence of "profane" days, with rest on the "sacred" day at their end. It was now a movement from Mount Tabor into the world, from the world into the "day without evening" of the world to come. Every day, every hour acquired now an importance, a gravity it could not have had before: Each day was now to be a *step* in this movement, a moment of decision and witness, a time of ultimate meaning. Sunday therefore was not a "sacred" day to be "observed" apart from all other days and opposed to them. It did not interrupt time with a "timeless" mystical ecstasy. It was not a "break" in an otherwise meaningless sequence of days and nights. By remaining one of the ordinary days, and yet by revealing itself through the eucharist as the eighth and first day, it gave all days their true meaning. It made the time of this world a time of the *end,* and it made it also the time of the *beginning.*

Alexander
Schmemann

O N every Lord's Day come together and break bread and give thanks, first confessing your sins so that your sacrifice may be pure. Anyone at variance with a neighbor must not join you, until they are reconciled, lest your sacrifice be defiled.

A Church Manual
Second century

B Y a tradition handed down from the apostles and having its origin from the very day of Christ's resurrection, the church celebrates the paschal mystery every eighth day, which, with good reason, bears the name of the Lord's Day or Sunday. For on this day Christ's faithful must gather together so that, by hearing the word of God and taking part in the eucharist, they may call to mind the passion, the resurrection, and the glorification of the Lord Jesus and may thank God, who "has begotten them again unto a living hope through the resurrection of Jesus Christ from the dead" (1 Peter 1:3). Hence the Lord's Day is the first holyday of all and should be proposed to the devotion of the faithful and taught to them in such a way that it may become in fact a day of joy and of freedom from work. Other celebrations, unless they be truly of greatest importance, shall not have precedence over the Sunday, the foundation and core of the whole liturgical year.

*Constitution on the
Sacred Liturgy*

I N the course of the Christian centuries, Sunday has remained a stable point of reference, lending a fixed rhythm to Christian lives lived in widely different circumstances of time and place. Yet, for all its stability, it has come to mean many different things. This was true even in the early centuries, as the different names given to Sunday attest; "the first day of the week," "the Lord's day," "the eighth day," to mention the most common. Later, in the middle ages, it came also to be spoken of analogously as the Sabbath. Each of these names, plus the kind of observances considered appropriate for this day, reflect different insights into the mystery of Sunday.

The term "mystery" is deliberate. Here, as in the liturgy generally, it is used to mean a symbol or sacrament—not something we cannot understand so much as something we can only understand by living with it and can never explain exhaustively. Sunday is not just a day, not even a day apart: It is a symbol, a sacrament, of our life with God in Christ. Like the other sacraments, Sunday offers us insight into the life we live together in the unity of the Spirit and itself draws us into that life. Like the other sacraments, it has undergone quite astonishing changes of form and celebration in the course of time. But, as is also the case with other sacraments, these changes in form—despite the limitations inevitably associated with each of them—offer us different insights into the mystery we live.

Mark Searle

S INCE it is Sunday, at dawn they assemble for the liturgy in the major church built by Constantine and located on Golgotha behind the Cross; and whatever is done all over customarily on Sunday is done here.

Egeria
Fourth century

W HEN all work is brought to a standstill, the candles are lit. Just as creation began with the word, "Let there be light!" so does the celebration of creation begin with the kindling of lights. It is the woman who ushers in the joy and sets up the most exquisite symbol, light, to dominate the atmosphere of the home.

And the world becomes a place of rest. An hour arrives like a guide, and raises our minds above accustomed thoughts. People assemble to welcome the wonder of the seventh day, while the Sabbath sends out its presence over the fields, into our homes, into our hearts. It is a moment of resurrection of the dormant spirit in our souls.

Refreshed and renewed, attired in festive garments, with candles nodding dreamily to unutterable expectations, to intuitions of eternity, some of us are overcome with a feeling, as if almost all they would say would be like a veil. There is not enough grandeur in our souls to be able to unravel in words the knot of time and eternity. One should like to sing for all people, for all generations. Some people chant the greatest of all songs: The Song of Songs. What ancient attachment, what an accumulation of soul is flowing in their chant! It is a chant of love for God, a song of passion, nostalgia and tender apology.

A thought has blown the market place away. There is a song in the wind and joy in the trees. The Sabbath arrives in the world, scattering a song in the silence of the night: Eternity utters a day. Where are the words that could compete with such might?

Abraham Joshua
Heschel

W HAT exactly is a feast day? Just as one can say that an altar is a piece of earth raised a little towards heaven, so one can say of a feast day that it is a piece of time which touches eternity.

Joseph Jungmann

C HRIST has said "Let the dead bury their dead." The liturgical year is not a mere series of feasts intended to fix our minds on a dead past. It is, as Pope Pius XII told us, "Christ himself, living on in his church, still pursuing that path of boundless mercy which, 'going about and doing good,' he began to tread during his life on earth. This he did in order that the souls of all might come into contact with his mysteries and, so to speak, live by them." God is still kneading the dough of human nature and making it rise today. It is by means of the liturgy that God unites the leavened mass with the Godhead. That is why the church, at Matins on the feast of the Epiphany, sings, "*Today* the church is united to her heavenly bridegroom." And at Easter she sings, "*This* is the day of the Lord's making: a day of triumph and rejoicing."

A. G. Martimort

S OMEONE may remonstrate, "Does not everyone know what a festival is, anyhow?" The question is not altogether irrelevant. However, "If no one asks me, I know: If I wish to explain it to one that asks, I know not." This sentence from St. Augustine's *Confessions,* although written in relation to something else, is highly applicable to the concept of festivity. The problem is to put into words what everyone means and knows.

Nowadays, however, we are forcefully "asked" both what a festival is and, even more, what the psychological prerequisites are for celebrating one. "The trick is not to arrange a festival, but to find people who can *enjoy* it." The man who jotted down this aphorism nearly one hundred years ago was Friedrich Nietzsche; his genius, as this sentence once again illustrates, lay to no small degree in that seismographic sensitivity to what was to come. The implication is that festivity in general is in danger of extinction, for arrangements alone do not make a festival. Since Nietzsche's day it has become a more or less standard matter to connect the "misery of this present age" with "human's incapacity for festivity."   Joseph Pieper

L ITURGY then is no etherial intangible, it is absolute as birth and judgment and death. It is easier to deny life than grace. Our yearning for the coming of the newborn child into the crib of our hearts is not empty sentiment; underlying it is the solid truth of the "new birth of the only-begotten in the flesh." So, too, the second coming of Christ in power and glory is no pious daydream but a pledged reality through the Mass-mystery; for in the Christmas liturgy we joyfully and confidently approach our future judge as well as God's only-begotten Son (oration of the Vigil of Christmas). The sacramental interpretation of the Mass liturgy sees it as a veritable treasury of grace, the sun embodying and emitting all the rays proper to the work of redemption, be they commemorative, eschatological or sacramentally prognostic.

Through the liturgy, then, we receive our only true treasure, the precious pearl of divine life. The church's year is indeed a year of grace.   Pius Parsch

L ET the Catholic who reads this work be on guard against that coldness of faith, and that want of love, which have well-nigh turned into an object of indifference that admirable cycle of the church, which heretofore was, and always ought to be, the joy of the people, the source of light to the learned, and the book of the humblest of the faithful.

The reader will rightly infer, from what we have said, that the object we have in view is not, in any way, to publish some favourite or clever method of our own with regard to the mysteries of the ecclesiastical year, nor to make them subjects for eloquence, philosophy, or intellectual fancy. We have but one aim, and we humbly ask of God that we may attain it; it is to serve as interpreter to the church, in order thus to enable the faithful to follow it in its prayer of each mystic season, nay, of each day and hour. God forbid that we should ever presume to put our human thoughts side by side with those which our Lord Jesus Christ, who is the wisdom of God, dictates by the Holy Ghost to this well-beloved bride the church! All that we would do is to show what is the spirit which the Holy Ghost has put into each of the several periods of the liturgical year; and for this purpose, to study attentively the most ancient and venerable liturgies, and embody in our explanation the sentiments of the holy fathers and the oldest and most approved liturgists. With these helps, we hope to give to the faithful the flowers of ecclesiastical prayer, and thus unite, as far as possible, practical usefulness with the charm of variety. . . .

There is not a single point of Christian doctrine which, in the course of the liturgical year, is not brought forward, nay, is not inculcated with that authority and unction wherewith the church has so deeply impregnated its words and its eloquent rites. The faith of the believer is thus enlightened more and more each year; the theological *sensus* is formed in us; prayer leads us to science. Mysteries continue to be mysteries; but their brightness becomes so vivid, that the mind and heart are enchanted, and we begin to imagine what a joy the eternal sight of these divine beauties will produce in us, Prosper Gueranger   when the glimpse of them through the clouds is such a Nineteenth century   charm to us.

I T is true that the myths and symbols of archaic worship have to some extent left their mark on Christian symbolism since the days when the gospel was preached in the world of Greece and Rome. Nevertheless, all Christianity that is true to its origins preserves the purity and simplicity of that eschatological vision which makes time utterly transparent, for all time has now become "the time of the end."

But in proportion as we regard our Christian life as the canonization of merely temporal and social patterns, and as we place our hopes in a Christianity fully rooted and established not in Christ himself, regardless of time, but in time "with the approval of Christ," we will have an entirely different concept of liturgy and of Christianity, we will make our worship the reflection and glorification of the institutional structures in which we imagine our temporal hope to be made secure.

Liturgical time loses its meaning when it becomes simply the complacent celebration of *status quo,* and if the "present" of liturgy is merely the "given" situation in which we find our human security. The paradox of liturgical time is that it is humanly insecure, seeking its peace together outside the structures of all that is established, visible and familiar, in the hope of a kingdom that is not seen. It is that hope and that alone that makes Christ present among us. Outside that eschatological hope there is no meaning and no dynamism in liturgical worship.

Thomas Merton

IT may well be that one of the reasons why so many people are attracted to the various crafts today is that the craftsperson has a style of life that is marked by steady rhythms and engaged with elemental forces. There is a time for the labor of digging and mixing earths, a time for the heat of fire, and a time for contemplating what is done. The moment of turning a pot still warm in the hand to judge the result of labor is both the apex of a creative cycle and a gentle reminder that the next cycle is soon to begin.

Cecilia Davis
Cunningham

WE are always *between* morning and evening, *between* Sunday and Sunday, *between* Easter and Easter, *between* the two comings of Christ. The experience of time as *end* gives an absolute importance to whatever we do *now,* makes it final, decisive. The experience of time as *beginning* fills all our time with joy, for it adds to it the "co-efficient" of eternity: "I shall not die but live and declare the works of the Lord." We are at work in the world, and this work—in fact, any work—if analyzed in terms of the world in itself, becomes meaningless, futile, irrelevant. In every city in the world there is each morning a rush of clean people getting to work. And every evening there is a rush of the same people, now tired and dirty, going in the opposite direction. . . .

For centuries we have preached to the hurrying people: Your daily *rush* has no meaning, yet accept it—and you will be rewarded in *another* world by an eternal rest. But God revealed and offers us eternal Life and not eternal rest. And God revealed this eternal Life in the midst of time—and of its *rush*—as its secret meaning and goal. And thus God made time, and our work in it, into the *sacrament of the world to come,* the liturgy of fulfillment and ascension. It is when we have reached the very end of the world's self-sufficiency that it *begins* again for us as the material of the sacrament that we are to fulfill in Christ.

Alexander
Schmemann

I am speaking against some contemporary attempts to make liturgical celebrations a kind of instant Day of God, attempts to act out in liturgy a realized eschatology. Liturgy does, in fact, offer time and room and invitation to play and act as if the kingdom were now. But I hope that there is also always place for discontent (to be not only implied but also articulated), for a sense of the hiddenness and the not-yetness of a kingdom which has come now in a crucified man and in the proclamation of the crucified. "After all, you have died! Your life is hidden now with Christ in God. When Christ our life appears, then you shall appear with him in glory" (Colossians 3:3 – 4).

And I hope that whatever liturgy we celebrate has a revolutionary sense and meaning, a revolutionary character in this world, so that our celebrations do not leave this world essentially untouched but cry out for God's kingdom to come to this created world and for at last God's justice to be done. So that no bruised reed is broken and no smoldering wick is crushed, and so that the coastlands, all the nations of the earth that wait for God's law may see God's rule at last.

Such must be our liturgy. Our liturgy must be a place where our longing can be appropriately expressed. And all the while the sense of liturgy must also be the joy that God is in our lament, is with us in our lament, and even in our death and in the contingency of our life. This meal, we say of the eucharist, is the *eschatological banquet.* But this eschatological banquet, this feast to which all the world is invited without exception, at which enemies sit down and become friends, in which all barriers are overcome and all hungers satisfied—this is still a feast in the body and blood of the hungry one with us.

Gordon Lathrop

L IKEWISE, the Lord's Supper is not to be regarded in terms of mystery and cult, but eschatologically. The congregation at the table is not in possession of the sacral presence of the Absolute, but is a waiting, expectant congregation seeking communion with the coming Lord. Thus Christianity is to be understood as the community of those who on the ground of the resurrection of Christ wait for the kingdom of God and whose life is determined by this expectation.

Jürgen Moltmann

O F course, right then, he should have urged her to put off the end of her telling; and he was about to do so, to suggest that now, in the time left before the mourners were due, she should rest, gather herself.... He'd go for a bit of a walk down the lane, give her a chance to be alone.

But she got ahead of him by speaking first, and with a commanding strength: "One thing I've learned, Father—that in this life it's best to keep the then and the now and the what's-to-be as close together in your thoughts as you can. It's when you let gaps creep in, when you separate out the intervals and dwell on them, that you can't bear the sorrow." And, as if to prove her point: "It was lingering over the first time we saw the cattle-fold that got me off."

"You're right of course about joining the pieces of life together," he said quietly. "It's the hardest part, keeping the view whole."

Jeannette Haien

ALL art is at once surface and symbol.
Those who go beneath the surface do so at their peril.
Those who read the symbol do so at their peril.
It is the spectator, and not life, that art really mirrors.
Diversity of opinion about a work of art shows that the work
    is new, complex, and vital.
When critics disagree the artist is in accord with himself.
We can forgive a man for making a useful thing as long
    as he does not admire it. The only excuse for making a
    useless thing is that one admires it intensely.
All art is quite useless.

Oscar Wilde

As I go on living and working in the way of vulnerability, I have been repairing your Cowley cloak, which you've had since we were newly married. You wore it in cold weather to go over to the chapel to say the offices. It's riddled with moth holes, but it feels wonderful to wear, like a blanket that folds me but doesn't hobble me. Besides, to me it feels like being wrapped in you. So I badly want to wear it too, as a prayer shawl and the mantle of Elijah.

But here's the good bit. It is *so* moth-eaten, really. There would be so many darns it would look awful, however neatly done. So I have been crocheting woolen flowers to decorate the moth-holes. Lots of maroon roses and purple daisies and deep blue borage flowers and dark green leaves. But there as so many holes! When I hold it open against the light it looks like the starry sky. Indeed, I think working on it is making more come. So I hear my mother and all sensible people including myself saying that it's a terrible waste of time and work. Why don't I put this energy into a new bit of cloth that will last?

The thing is, though, this cloak is a celebration of "holey-ness" and flaws. The more I work it, the more I wear it, the more tattered it will get and the more flowers will grow there to proclaim vulnerability as the power in healing and the aim of prayer, and the connection that is blessing will be made through the holes.

Janet Gaden

S PITS of glitter in lowgrade ore,
precious stones too poorly surrounded for harvest,
to all things not worth the work
of having,

brush oak on a sharp slope, for example,
the balk tonnage of woods-lodged boulders,
the irreparable desert,
drowned river mouths, lost shores where

the winged and light-footed go,
take creosote bush that possesses
ground nothing else will have,
to all things and for all things

crusty or billowy with indifference,
for example, incalculable, irremovable water
of fluvio-glacial deposits
larch or dwarf aspen in the least breeze
    sometimes shiver in —

suddenly the salvation of waste betides,
the peerlessly unsettled seas that shape the continents,
take the gales wasting and in waste over
Antarctica and the sundry high shoals of ice,

for the inexcusable (the worthless abundant) the
merely tiresome, the obviously unimprovable,
to these and for these and for their undiminishment
the poets will yelp and hoot forever

probably,
rank as weeds themselves and just as abandoned:
nothing useful is of lasting value:
A. R. Ammons   dry wind only is still talking among the oldest stones.

IN the Christian ritual everything is open to the infinite appeal of love. Even the initiation, the baptism, like the faith which it represents and sanctions, is for all: Only those who exclude themselves are excluded; this election is essentially catholic. But at the beginning stands the mystery of God's own life, and finally there remains a true human mystery: what we call the secret of the heart, the authentic response of the human will to the divine summons. For no one knows whether he or she merits praise or blame. Christian life does not rest upon any certainty as to our own state of grace, and surely we cannot discern the state of our neighbor's soul.

All the rest is visible, and in its perpetual visibility more baffling to our complex souls than the "artistic" chiaroscuro of any human drama. The Christian mystery is more mysterious than any other: It is the very mystery of God, reflected in the secret of conscience. Otherwise, all is clarity. As Barrès once
Jean de Menasce   said of El Greco, it is a mystery in broad daylight.

COMMENTATORS have been puzzled at the passage in the *amidah* ("the silent prayer"), *"for thou hearest in mercy the prayer of every mouth."* We would expect the phrase to be *"the prayer of every heart."* But the passage, we are told, is intended to remind us that it is the mercy of God to accept even prayers that come only from the mouth as lip-service, without inner devotion. However, this remark in no way denies the principle that *kavanah,* or inner participation, is indispensable to prayer. It is a principle that found a precise expression in the medieval saying: "Prayer without *kavanah* is like a body without a soul."

Yet, what is the nature of *kavanah* or inner participation? Is it paying attention to the context of the fixed texts? Thinking? Prayer is not thinking. To the thinker, God is an object; to the one who prays, God is the subject. Awaking in the presence of God, we strive not to acquire objective knowledge, but to deepen the mutual allegiance of ourselves and God. What we want is not to know God, but to be known to God; not to form judgments about God, but to be judged by God; not to make the world an object of our mind, but to let the world come to God's attention, to augment God's, rather than our knowledge. We endeavor to disclose ourselves to the Sustainer of all, rather than to enclose the world in ourselves.

Abraham Joshua Heschel

RITUAL is not to be seen as a content to which people must comply, but as a structure within which they can pulsate and pirouette in unprescribed ways. Ritual should lure people into festive fantasy, put them in touch with the deepest longings of the race, help them to step into the parade of history, and ignite their capacity for creation.

Harvey Cox

THE eighteenth-century Hasidic Jews had more sense, and more belief. One Hasidic slaughterer, whose work required invoking the Lord, bade a tearful farewell to his wife and children every morning before he set out for the slaughterhouse. He felt, every morning, that he would never see any of them again. For every day, as he himself stood with his knife in his hand, the words of his prayer carried him into danger. After he called on God, God might notice and destroy him before he had time to utter the rest, "Have mercy."

Another Hasid, a rabbi, refused to promise a friend to visit him the next day: "How can you ask me to make such a promise? This evening I must pray and recite 'Hear, O Israel.' When I say these words, my soul goes out to the utmost rim of life. . . . Perhaps I shall not die this time either, but how can I now promise to do something at a time after the prayer?"

Annie Dillard

M AN, my friends," said General Loewenhielm, "is frail and foolish. We have all of us been told that grace is to be found in the universe. But in our human foolishness and short-sightedness we imagine divine grace to be finite. For this reason we tremble . . ." Never till now had the General stated that he trembled; he was genuinely surprised and even shocked at hearing his own voice proclaim the fact. "We tremble before making our choice in life, and after having made it again tremble in fear of having chosen wrong. But the moment comes when our eyes are opened, and we see and realize that grace is infinite. Grace, my friends, demands nothing from us but that we shall await it with confidence and acknowledge it in gratitude. Grace, brothers, makes no conditions and singles out none of us in particular; grace takes us all to its bosom and proclaims general amnesty. See! that which we have chosen is given us, and that which we have refused is, also and at the same time, granted us. Ay, that which we have rejected is poured upon us abundantly. For mercy and truth have met together, and righteousness and bliss have kissed one another!"

Of what happened later in the evening nothing definite can here be stated. None of the guests later on had any clear remembrance of it. They only knew that the rooms had been filled with a heavenly light, as if a number of small halos had blended into one glorious radiance. Taciturn old people received the gift of tongues; ears that for years had been almost deaf were opened to it. Time itself had merged into eternity. Long after midnight the windows of the house shone like gold, and golden song flowed out into the winter air.   Isak Dinesen

WHEN was the last genuine banquet held by your church? Neither Isaiah nor our Lord speaks of a church supper, of chicken and peas, meat loaf and potatoes, beef and beer, but of a banquet.

The congregation was approaching their centennial and a committee was formed. All agreed there should be a dinner. The older members assumed it would be in the church assembly room, though perhaps the somewhat worn and faded tablecloths might be used, and even a local person hired to cook rather than doing the usual potluck.

Then the chair, a new African American member, suggested a hotel: a real banquet. The veterans were shocked. Wouldn't that cost money? The young people loved the idea: they wanted a banquet too. After hiring a baby sitter they were not about to go to a boring church meal. The conversation was lively, and finally, the banquet won.

More people came than ever before had come. Men who were dull came alive and women reveled. Perhaps in another hundred years, they would do it again.   David K. McMillan

I return to the story of *Babette's Feast*. Most of what we see in the film is simply the day-in, day-out existence of a little group of not very attractive people, to whom two women minister with varying degrees of success. Into their midst comes Babette, a gifted woman who knows how to do things: how to shop with marvelous thrift, how to cook tasty meals, how to "shush" the quarrels of these old people, how to get them to sing again, though in an off-key and distracted manner. Now, I dare say that many of us and many of the communities of faith we represent would see ourselves as called to do for the old among us what the two women did before Babette arrived—hard, generous, caring, loving work that makes a substantial difference to the old who are in their care. But no more.

I see things differently. We need to provide "banquets"— powerful rituals of some sort—in which transformation occurs. In many ways the old in our midst, and they are many, take the measure of our life together. Our willingness to go beyond their need for physical care, to admit that they are called to self-transcendence, to wrestle with their in-common lives and to try to address their needs in trans-forming rituals, signifies events of grace.

Henry C. Simmons

WE enter a house on Thanksgiving day and we can "smell where to go," to the feast and its fragrance. For there is no feasting without fragrance. The feasting of a child at its mother's breast, the feasting of a wife at her hus-band's body, the feasting of a family at table—all these feasts are replete with the perfume of that which is shared and of those who share it. That is why the apostle Paul can write to the Corinthians of the fragrance of their union with Christ, calling those who are baptized into that union, the incense, the good aroma of Christ for God. . . .

So where is this "vital fragrance" in the Sunday assembly? Where is the fragrance of feasting at the feast of the eucha-rist? Where is the odor of the beloved, leading us, evoking memory and desire? All of us who celebrate the liturgy of word and of table should wind up soaked in the juices and smelling of the good work of worship. We should emerge bearing the sign of who and what we are, "the good aroma of Christ for God" (2 Corinthians 2:15).

Melissa Musick
Nussbaum

CONSIDER how great is the honor you have been granted; consider how awesome is the table you enjoy. What even angels cannot see without trembling, what they dare not look upon because of its shimmering brightness—that we are fed by; that we are joined to, making us one body and one flesh with Christ. . . .

Through these mysteries, Christ joins himself to each one of the faithful. Those he begets [in baptism], he nourishes with his own bodily being . . . proving to you once more that he has taken on your very flesh. Let us not grow blasé about being counted worthy of so much love and honor. Haven't you ever noticed how eagerly a baby seizes its mother's breast, how ravenously it presses its lips onto the nipple? With the same eagerness, we ought to approach this table and the nipple of this spiritual cup. Or rather, with even greater enthusiasm, like babies at the breast, let us draw out the Spirit's grace.

John Chrysostom

I'VE known rivers:
I've known rivers ancient as the world and older than the
    flow of human blood in human veins.

My soul has grown deep like the rives.

I bathed in the Euphrates when dawns were young.
I built my hut near the Congo and it lulled me to sleep.
I looked upon the Nile and raised the pyramids above it.
I heard the singing of the Mississippi when Abe Lincoln
    went down to New Orleans, and I've seen its muddy
    bosom turn all golden in the sunset.

I've know rivers.
Ancient, dusky rivers.

My soul has grown deep like the rivers.

Langston Hughes

EVERYTHING was a ritual. Doing the dishes, mowing the lawn, baking bread, quilting, canning, hanging out the laundry, picking fresh produce, weeding. Friday: house-cleaning; Saturday: mowing the lawn; Monday: washing. Emma, Lydia, and Miriam, three generations of women living side by side, knew exactly what had to be done and in what order. Nothing had to be explained.

No distinction was made between the sacred and the every-day. Five minutes in the early morning and five minutes in the evening were devoted to prayer. The rest of the day was spent living their beliefs. Their life was all one piece. It was all sacred—and all ordinary.

Sue Bender

NEVER say, then, as some say: "The kingdom of matter is worn out, matter is dead": till the very end of time matter will always remain young, exuberant, sparkling, new-born for those who are willing.

Never say, "Matter is accursed, matter is evil": for there has come one who said, "You will drink poisonous draughts and they shall not harm you," and again, "Life shall spring forth out of death," and then finally, the words which spell my definitive liberation, "This is my body."

Purity does not lie in separation form, but in a deeper pen-etration into the universe. It is to be found in the love of that unique, boundless Essence which penetrates the inmost depths of all things and there, from within those depths, deeper than the mortal zone where individuals and multi-tudes struggle, works upon them and moulds them. Purity lies in a chaste contact with that which is "the same in all."

Oh, the beauty of spirit as it rises up adorned with all the riches of the earth!

Bathe yourself in the ocean of matter; plunge into it where it is deepest and most violent; struggle in its currents and drink of its waters. For it cradled you long ago in your pre-conscious existence; and it is that ocean that will raise you up to God.

Pierre Teilhard de Chardin

E ARTH's crammed with heaven,
And every common bush afire with God;
But only he who sees takes off his shoes;
The rest sit round it and pluck blackberries.

Elizabeth Barrett
Browning
Nineteenth century

C HRISTIANITY is not reconciliation with death. It is the revelation of death, and it reveals death because it is the revelation of Life. Christ is this Life. And only if Christ is Life is death what Christianity proclaims it to be, namely the enemy to be destroyed, and not a "mystery" to be explained. Religion and secularism, by explaining death, give it a "status," a rationale, make it "normal." Only Christianity proclaims it to be *abnormal* and, therefore, truly horrible. At the grave of Lazarus Christ wept, and when his own hour to die approached, "he began to be sore amazed and very heavy." In the light of Christ, *this* world, this *life* are lost and are beyond mere "help," not because there is fear of death in them, but because they have accepted and normalized death. To accept God's world as a cosmic cemetery which is to be abolished and replaced by an "other world" which looks like a cemetery ("eternal rest") and to call this religion, to live in a cosmic cemetery and to "dispose" every day of thousands of corpses and to get excited about a "just society" and to be happy!—this is the fall of humanity. It is not our immorality or our crimes that reveal us as a fallen being; it is our "positive ideal"—religious or secular—and our satisfaction with this ideal. This fall, however, can be truly revealed only by Christ, because only in Christ is the *fullness of life* revealed to us, and death, therefore, becomes "awful," the very fall from life, the enemy. It is *this world* (and not any "other world"), it is *this life* (and not some "other life") that were given to us to be a sacrament of the divine presence, given as communion with God, and it is only through this world, this life, by "transforming" them into communion with God that humanity *was to be.* The horror of death is, therefore, not in its being the "end" and not in physical destruction. By being separation from the world of life, it is *separation from God.* The dead cannot glorify God. It is, in other words, when Christ reveals Life to us that we can hear the Christian message about death as the enemy of God. It is when Life weeps at the grave of the friend, when it contemplates the horror of death, that the victory over death begins.

Alexander
Schmemann

IT is plain that such a religion as Christianity, which has for its object the worship of the Divine self-revealed in history, the Logos incarnate in time and space—which seeks and finds God self-given, in and through the littleness of the manger, and the shamefulness of the cross—is closely bound up with a sacramental interpretation of life. Christ, as Bérulle said so deeply and so boldly, is "himself the major sacrament"; the visible sign of the nature of the eternal God, and the medium of that eternal God's self-giving. And the church, as his mystical body, the organ of his continued presence, lives with a sacramental life from which the reality and power of the specific Christian sacraments proceed, and which indeed gives to them their credentials. This precision, this apparent canalizing of a grace and power which are felt by the religious soul to be boundless in generosity and unconditioned in action, and operative throughout the whole of life, repels many spiritual minds. They can easily accept a diffused sacramentalism; but reject the notion of a special and ordained channel of grace. Nevertheless the distinctness of the Holy will never be sufficiently realized by us, unless God's self-giving be apprehended as coming to us, the creature, in a special sense by particular paths; held sacred, and kept for God alone. And this means sacraments. The deep conviction of the Platonist that everything is a shadow and outward sign of a deeper and more enduring reality, is indeed precious as far as it goes; and is justified in those rare moments when the lovely veil is lifted and we catch a glimpse of greater loveliness behind. But this can never be enough for Christianity; which discloses a real God to real persons by means of a real life and death in space and time. And here the law of belief must be the law of worship too.

Evelyn Underhill

THE man Jesus, as the personal visible realization of the divine grace of redemption, is *the* sacrament, the primordial sacrament, because this man, the Son of God himself, is intended by the Father to be in his humanity the only way to the actuality of redemption. "For there is one God, and one mediator of God and men, the man Christ Jesus." Personally to be approached by the man Jesus was, for his contemporaries, an invitation to a personal encounter with the life-giving God, because personally that man was the Son of God. Human encounter with Jesus is therefore the sacrament of the encounter with God, or of the religious life as a theologal attitude of existence towards God. Jesus' human redeeming acts are therefore a "sign and cause of grace." "Sign" and "cause" of salvation are not brought together here as two elements fortuitously conjoined. Human bodiliness is human interiority itself in visible form.

Now because the inward power of Jesus' will to redeem and of his human love is God's own saving power realized in human form, the human saving acts of Jesus are the divine bestowal of grace itself realized in visible form; that is to say they cause what they signify; they are sacraments.

Edward Schillebeeckx

SACRAMENTS do not exist for God's sake; God transcends all signs and all means. They only exist for our sake because we are creatures of body and spirit and because of the fall. *Sacramenta propter homines.* Compare this theological adage with the words of the *Credo: Qui propter nos homines et propter nostram salutem descendit de caelis.* It is for us and for our salvation that the Son of God, God of God, light of light, came down from heaven.

A.-M. Roguet

CHRISTIANS have not hesitated to use every human art in their celebration of the saving work of God in Jesus Christ, although in every historical period they have been influenced, at times inhibited, by cultural circumstances. In the resurrection of the Lord, all things are made new. Wholeness and healthiness are restored, because the reign of sin and death is conquered. Human limits are still real and we must be conscious of them. But we must also praise God and give God thanks with the human means we have available. God does not need liturgy; people do, and people have only their own arts and styles of expression with which to celebrate.

Environment and Art in Catholic Worship

ALL of this suggests to me that in the sacrament of the sick what is at stake is the sacramentality of sickness itself, or, perhaps it would be better to say, the mystery which is revealed in the sick person who lives through this experience. In other words, the accent is not on healing, nor on forgiving, nor on preparing for death. It is on the sick person, who through this experience discovers God in a particular way and reveals this to the community. All the other factors enter in, but they are related to this as organizing centre.

David N. Power

DESPITE common opinion to the contrary, symbols are neither nostalgic remembrances of the past nor familiar reminders of things we already know. Symbols are not things people invent and interpret, but realities that "make" and interpret a people. What we need today is not so much "better symbols," but a willingness to let ourselves be grasped and explored by them. For a symbol is not an object to be manipulated through mime and memory, but an environment to be inhabited. Symbols are places to live, breathing spaces that help us discover what possibilities life offers.

To put the matter succinctly: every symbol deals with a new discovery and every symbol is an open-ended action, not a closed-off object. By engaging in symbols, by inhabiting their environment, people discover new horizons for life, new values and motivations.... Because they are open-ended actions symbols can expand, grow and deepen. To think of symbols as changeless reminders of irreformable truths is nonsense.

Symbols are supple, flexible, pliant. Their relation to people is *reciprocal:* Symbols disclose new potentials for human life, but they are also shaped and refined by the changing circumstances of that life. We might call this the *"principle of symbolic reciprocity":* symbols both influence and are influenced by the very interactions that evoke them.   Nathan Mitchell

THERE is nothing wrong with inventing rituals. All rituals were at one time invented by someone. But if we want to express our deepest feelings to ourselves and to others, ritual must have a social dimension. And if we are to be in touch with what others have sensed in the dim past, or if we want to pass on our experience to the future, the ritual must have a historical dimension as well. Furthermore, even to express our deepest feelings to ourselves, we need a ritual, just as we need a language even to talk to ourselves. Ritual does for movement what language does for sound, transforms it from the inchoate into the expressive. Therefore an idiosyncratic ritual is ultimately frustrating and self-defeating.   Harvey Cox

WHEN we enter the world of worship, we enter a world which has many of the characteristics of an artistic creation. Much crude and unedifying controversy would die away, were this fact commonly admitted and the poetry and music which enter so largely into expressive worship were recognized as indications of its essential character. The true object of our worship cannot be directly apprehended by us. "No one has seen God at any time." The representative pattern, the suggestive symbol, the imaginative projection too—all these must be called into play and their limitations humbly accepted if the limited creature is to enter into communion with the Holy and so develop a capacity for adoring love. But the difficulty of our situation is this: None of these devices will be effective unless the worshiper takes them seriously, far more seriously indeed than in their naked factualness they deserve. This is the element in expressive worship which is so puzzling to those who stand outside it. Why, for instance, this devout contemplation of a rather bad picture, or punctual recitation of a rather silly prayer?   Evelyn Underhill

Y OU were led to the holy pool of divine baptism, as Christ was carried from the cross to the sepulchre which is before our eyes. And each of you was asked whether you believed in the name of the Father, and of the Son, and of the Holy Spirit, and you made that saving confession, and descended three times into the water, and ascended again; here also covertly pointing by a figure at the three-days burial of Christ. For as our Savior passed three days and three nights in the heart of the earth, so you also in your first ascent out of the water represented the first day of Christ in the earth, and by your descent, the night; for as those who are in the night see no more, but those who are in the day remain in the light, so in descending you saw nothing as in the night, but in ascending again you were as in the day. And at the self-same moment, you died and were born; and that water of salvation was at once your grave and your mother. And what Solomon spoke of others will suit you also: "There is a time to be born and a time to die"; but to you, on the contrary, the time to die is also the time to be born; and one and the same season brings about both of these, and your birth went hand in hand with your death.

O strange and inconceivable thing! We did not really die, we were not really buried, we were not really crucified and raised again, but our imitation was merely in a figure, while our salvation is in reality. Christ was actually crucified, and actually buried, and truly rose again; and all these things have been vouchsafed to us, that we, by imitation communicating in his sufferings, might gain salvation in reality. O surpassing loving-kindness! Christ received the nails in his undefiled hands and feet, and endured anguish; while to me without suffering or toil, by the fellowship of his pain he vouchsafes salvation.

Let no one then suppose that baptism is merely the grace of remission of sins, or further, that of adoption, as John's baptism bestowed only the remission of sins. Indeed we know full well, that as it purges our sins, and conveys to us the gift of the Holy Spirit, so also it is the counterpart of Christ's sufferings. For, for this cause Paul cried aloud and says: "Know you not that as many of us as were baptized into Christ Jesus were baptized into his death? Therefore we are buried with him by baptism into death."

Cyril of Jerusalem
Fourth century

I s that everything?"

"I don't know how to put it, Father, but I feel—tired of my religion. It seems to mean nothing to me. I've tried to love God, but—" he made a gesture which the priest could not see, turned sideways through the grille. "I'm not sure that I even believe."

"It's easy," the priest said, "to worry too much about that. Especially here. The penance I would give a lot of people if I could is six months' leave. The climate gets you down. It's easy to mistake tiredness for—well, disbelief."

"I don't want to keep you, Father. There are other people waiting. I know these are just fancies. But I feel—empty. Empty."

"That's sometimes the moment God chooses," the priest said. "Now go along with you and say a decade of your rosary."

"I haven't a rosary. At least . . . "

"Well, five Our Father's and five Hail Marys then." He began to speak the words of absolution, but the trouble is, Scobie thought, there's nothing to absolve. The words brought no sense of relief because there was nothing to relieve. They were a formula: the Latin words hustled together—a hocus pocus. He went out of the box and knelt down again, and this too was part of a routine. It seemed to him for a moment that God was too accessible. There was no difficulty in approaching Him. Like a popular demagogue He was open to the least of His followers at any hour. Looking up at the cross he thought, He even suffers in public.   Graham Greene

ONE who is convinced that symbol and reality are mutually exclusive should avoid the liturgy. Such a one should also avoid poetry, concerts and the theater, language, loving another person, and most other attempts at communicating with one's own kind. Symbol is reality at its most intense degree of being expressed. One resorts to symbol when reality swamps all other forms of discourse. This happens regularly when one approaches God with others, as in the liturgy. Symbol is thus as native to liturgy as metaphor is to language. One learns to live with symbol and metaphor or gives up the ability to speak or to worship communally.

Aidan Kavanagh

IT is precisely their rich multivalence that makes symbols to be symbols: They evoke not simply one sort of feeling, or one kind of mood, but a whole spectrum of experience. They touch the whole range of possible human response. Thus it does not matter that staying up late at night is one person's idea of a good time and another's idea of an ordeal. Ordeal and festivity are both common elements of a real vigil (remember, the word vigil simply means night watch or wake), and the symbols of the paschal vigil "work" precisely because they can touch those varied ranges of feeling and experience, as they allow for the sharing of such experience.

Ralph A. Keifer

A myth which is understood as a myth, but not removed or replaced, can be called a "broken myth." Christianity denies by its very nature any unbroken myth, because its presupposition is the first commandment: the affirmation of the ultimate as ultimate and the rejection of any kind of idolatry. All mythological elements in the Bible and doctrine and liturgy should be recognized as mythological, but they should be maintained in their symbolic form and not be replaced by scientific substitutes. For there is no substitute for the use of symbols and myths: They are the language of faith.

Paul Tillich

ASSEMBLING, dining, bathing, caressing can be taken up in the breath of the Spirit as the "matter," the stuff of the sacraments, precisely because they are already more than raw materials, more than utilitarian motions, more than fulfillers of biological need. They already transcend the "passing things of this world"— nine to five, greed, politics, petty plans and schemes and reasonable policies. These four gestures are already religious in the deepest sense, for it is such realities that find their fulfillment in the kingdom of heaven that is jubilant throng and flowing fountain, wedding feast and the wiping away of every tear....

Discussion has been so sterile, and experiment so fruitless, precisely because we continue to discourse about and act with sacraments as though they were *things,* and not for what they are— symbolic *gestures.* For example, it is not simply bread as material stuff or even as cultural artifact that constitutes the full eucharistic sign. It is bread prepared, given, broken and shared together. It is dining fraught with the tragedy of the crucifixion and transfigured by the glory of the resurrection, dining that proclaims the ultimate meaning of all bread shared with the poor, the ultimate meaning of all toasts at wakes, the ultimate thanksgiving of thanksgivings, the bread of life and the cup of salvation. Moreover, the gesture is not the utilitarian act of physical ingestion by itself; it is the whole act of gathering and conviviality, of admiring preparation, of gracious gestures of sharing.   Ralph A. Keifer

I don't pray because it makes sense to pray. I pray because my life doesn't make sense without prayer."

"Do you always pray in the same way, Jacob?"

Jacob spoke slowly. "Ritual gives form to passion. Passion without form consumes itself."

"The children said you told them 'Prayer is the path where there is none.' "

Jacob's eyes drew back their last curtain. "Yes. Prayer is a path where there is none, and ritual is prayer's vehicle."

Noah benShea

C HRISTIAN liturgy is a living icon, one composed primarily of persons, not signs. It is a peculiar image, in that it is a human, dynamic one. Its primary components are persons, not things, for we are a constituent part of it. It is not something outside of us which we contemplate, just as the dance has no subsistence apart from the dancers dancing, nor love apart from the lover loving the beloved.

Robert Taft

M ANY people reason quite the wrong way round about prayer, thinking that good actions and all sorts of preliminary measures render us capable of prayer. But quite the reverse is the case; it is prayer which bears fruit in good works and all the virtues. Those who reason so, take, incorrectly, the fruits and the results of prayer for the means of attaining it, and this is to depreciate the power of prayer. And it is quite contrary to holy scripture, for the Apostle Paul says, "I exhort therefore that first of all supplications be made" (1 Timothy 2:1). The first thing laid down in the apostle's words about prayer is that the work of prayer comes before everything else: "I exhort therefore that first of all . . ." Christians are bound to perform many good works, but before all else what they ought to do is to pray, for without prayer no other good work whatever can be accomplished. Without prayer they cannot find the way to the Lord, they cannot understand the truth, they cannot crucify the flesh with its passions and lusts, their hearts cannot be enlightened with the light of Christ, they cannot be savingly united to God.

The Way of the Pilgrim
Nineteenth century

THE Lord could do without our intercessions and our praise. Yet it is God's mystery to demand of us, God's co-workers, to keep on praying and never tire.

Let us be careful to seek the inner meaning of liturgical actions and strive to perceive, in signs accessible to people of flesh and blood, an invisible reality pertaining to the kingdom. But let us beware of multiplying these signs, being careful to preserve their simplicity—the token of their worth for the gospel.

The Rule of Taizé

THE liturgy of all rites has a lower temperature than what is usually called "popular" devotion. Liturgy is not effusive, not exuberant, never shouts, but sings, holds itself back like the Gregorian chant. In a famous weekday hymn at matins, composed by St. Gregory the Great, the church sings: "Laeti bibamus sobriam ebrietatem Spiritus" ("with joy let us drink the sober drunkenness of the Spirit"). "Sober drunkenness" seems a contradiction in terms, but its biblical prototype, the events of Pentecost, shows us what is really meant. It is a quiet rapture without shout and gesture; it is inebriation of the spirit, not drunkenness of the body dragging down the light of reason. All the rejoicing is "formed" by reason, and the emotions are on a level that will stimulate the reticent and restrain the exuberant.

In liturgical worship we are spared the embarrassing sight of unrestrained and naked emotion. There is a noble tact even in the greatest burst of joy or sadness. There is dignity which leaves the worshiper without shame after all is over, for nothing is more opposed to good liturgy than histrionics and theatrical display. What could there be more noble and moving than Jeremiah's lamentations sung during the vigils of mourning over Christ's passion and death?

Saying that the liturgy is sober and chaste and superior in content is not to be understood as an attempt to reserve the whole field of prayer, individual or communal, for the liturgy only. But the very sobriety and profundity of the liturgy are a challenge: The individual, as well as the congregation, has to fill these void vessels with their own personal contribution. Liturgy is either work, challenge, personal *"engagement,"* or it remains an empty house.

H. A. Reinhold

Τ HE rugged American individualist—impatient, as always, with the inconvenient *social* structure of Christian belief and praxis—prefers the friendly, pliable agendas of personal prayer to the intractable—often harsh and dreadful—demands of an ancient, historical and *public* cultus. For the liturgy of the Christian assembly stubbornly resists the manipulations of both politics and civil religion.

Nathan Mitchell

W HAT matters, therefore, is not whether God can be God without our worship. What is crucial is whether humans can survive as humans without worshiping. To withhold acknowledgment, to avoid celebration, to stifle gratitude, may prove as unnatural as holding one's breath.

John E. Burkhart

R EMEMBER, Lord, the people present here, and those who are absent for reasonable causes; replenish our storehouses with all manner of goods; preserve our marriages in peace and harmony; nourish the babes, instruct the youths, console the elderly; comfort the feeble-minded, collect the scattered, bring back the wandering and unite them to your holy, catholic and apostolic church. Free those who are bothered by unclean spirits; sail with those at sea, travel with the travelers, defend the widows, shield the orphans, preserve the prisoners, heal the sick. Remember, O God, those who stand before tribunals, and those in exile and in all kinds of tribulations and accidents, and all who need your great mercy; those who love us and those who hate us, and those who have begged us, unworthy though we be, to remember them in our prayers. Remember all your people, O Lord our God, and upon all pour forth your rich mercies, granting them everything they need for salvation. And those we have omitted through ignorance or forgetfulness or because of the multitude of their names, you yourself remember, O God who know the name and age of each, who have known each one from their mother's womb. For you, O Lord, are the helper of the helpless, the hope of the desperate, the saviour of the tempest-tossed, the harbor of voyagers, the physician of the sick. Become all things to all people, O you who know each person and their need, each house and its necessity. Preserve, O Lord, this city and every city and country place from plague, famine, earthquake, flood, fire, war, battle, invasion and riot.

Orthodox liturgy

WHY the Lord should ask us to pray, knowing what we need before we ask, may perplex us if we do not realize that our Lord and God does not want to know what we want (for the Lord cannot fail to know it) but wants us rather to exercise our desire through our prayers, so that we may be able to receive what God is preparing to give us. This gift is very great indeed, but our capacity is too small and limited to receive it. That is why we are told: "Enlarge your desires, do not bear the yoke with unbelievers."

The deeper our faith, the stronger our hope, the greater our desire, the larger will be our capacity to receive that gift, which is very great indeed. "No eye has seen it"; it has no sound. "It has not entered the human heart"; the human heart must enter into it.

In this faith, hope and love we pray always with unwearied desire. However, at set times and seasons we also pray to God in words, so that by these signs we may instruct ourselves and mark the progress we have made in our desire, and spur ourselves on to deepen it.

Augustine
Fifth century

O deep unknown, guttering candle,
  beloved nugget lodged
in the obscure heart's
last recess,
have mercy upon us.

We choose from the past, tearing morsels to feed
pride or grievance.
We live in terror
of what we know:

death, death, and the world's
death we imagine
        and cannot imagine,
we who may be
the first and the last witness.

We live in terror
of what we do not know,
in terror of not knowing,
of the limitless, through which freefalling
forever, our dread
sinks and sinks,

                or
        of the violent closure of all.

Yet our hope lies
in the unknown,
in our unknowing.

O deep, remote unknown,
O deep unknown,
Denise Levertov   Have mercy upon us.

OPEN the eyes of our hearts to know you, who alone are highest amid the highest, and ever abide holy amid the holy. You bring down the haughtiness of the proud, and scatter the devices of the people. You set up the lowly on high, and the lofty you cast down. Riches and poverty, death and life, are in your hand; you alone are the discerner of every spirit, and the God of all flesh. Your eyes behold the depths and survey the works of humankind; you are the aid of those in peril, the savior of them that despair, the creator and overseer of everything that has breath.... Deliver the afflicted, pity the lowly, raise the fallen, reveal yourself to the needy, heal the sick, and bring home your wandering people. Feed the hungry, ransom the captive, support the weak, comfort the fainthearted. Let all the nations of the earth know that you are God alone, that Jesus Christ is your child, and that we are your people and the sheep of your pasture.

Clement
First century

DAWDLING in the church
on one of those blank days,
I cannot think of much
that is good or wise.

My fingers idly stroke
the pew's polished grain
worn as smooth as silk
since Eighteen Forty-nine.

This unaltered air
has been here from the start,
thick with all the prayer
offered into it.

Shadows in the nave
and pictures on the glass
invite an elusive
simplicity of grace,

But I think of all
the mortal need brought here
by so many people
for so many years,

and freeze into a far
philosophical abyss
between what they prayed for
and what came to pass.

Kate Pratt

E VENING prayer is the appropriate place for common intercessions. After the day's work we pray God for the
blessing, peace, and safety of all Christendom; for our congregation; for the pastor; for the poor, the wretched, and
lonely; for the sick and dying; for our neighbors, for our own
folks at home and for our fellowship. When can we have
any deeper sense of God's power and working than in the
hour when our hands lay down their work and we commit
ourselves to the hands of God? When are we more ready for
the prayer of blessing, peace and preservation than the time
when our own activity ceases? When we grow weary, God
works. "Behold, the one who keeps Israel shall neither slumber nor sleep" (Psalm 121:4).

Dietrich Bonhoeffer

Kathleen Norris

T O me, monastic choirs, for all the discipline that is in
evidence, seem as open and free as country churches on
the Plains. Both monks and country people take for granted
that prayer works, and that it's worth doing. Why not relax
and enjoy it? Why not make it beautiful?

IS neighborhood repair a suitable manifestation of liturgical spirituality? Or blood donation for emergency use? But what would be more suitable? Does contemplative participation in the eucharistic mystery of Christ draw Christians out of their closed worlds, sending them more confidently to live among nonbelievers? Does contemplative participation make them more pious or more generous? Those who lament the loss of mystery occasioned by the liturgical reform may well have lost hold of their once-preferred manifestation of Christ's presence in a too-narrow cult of the tabernacle and the altar. But there is another manifestation of the mystery now available to the world outside the sanctuary: the people of God being built up day by day into the body of Christ for the world's healing and reconciliation.

There is no longer a medieval Christian Culture. Nor is there a post-Tridentine culture of Roman Catholicism to sustain the church's claim that it can show the world the way to salvation. The many cultural offers of salvation through self-promotion available at the end of the twentieth century make the demanding Christian message even less attractive as good news. Those of us who continue to believe in the paschal mystery as the only true offer of salvation must embody the mystery, incarnate it again for a skeptical world. To do so, we must always struggle to overcome our own faintheartedness and our own readiness to doubt. Corporate public ritual, say the theorists, gives participants an experience of ultimate mystery. Contemplative participation in the paschal mystery of Christ, say the people of Holy Wisdom, makes possible the appropriation of the identity the rites offer. Augustine instructed the church long ago: "Become who you are, the body of Christ." That, in sum, is the effect of liturgical spirituality.

Mary Collins

OF all the institutions in their lives, only the Catholic church has seemed aware of the fact that my mother and father are thinkers—persons aware of the experience of their lives. Other institutions—the nation's political parties, the industries of mass entertainment and communications, the companies that employed them—have all treated my parents with condescension. The church too has treated them badly when it attempted formal instruction. The homily at Sunday Mass, intended to give parishioners basic religious instruction, has often been poorly prepared and aimed at a childish listener. It has been the liturgical church that has excited my parents. In ceremonies of public worship, they have been moved, assured that their lives—all aspects of their lives, from waking to eating, from birth until death, all moments—possess great significance. Only the liturgy has encouraged them to dwell on the meaning of their lives. To think.

Richard Rodriguez

E VEN allowing for wide variation in the quality of rites and the manner of their celebration, we need to remind ourselves that sacraments always "work," and therefore what is claimed for them must be articulated within that certainty. That is to say, sacramental and liturgical realities are always and only that, and we do the theology of the liturgy no service by extravagant claims of extrinsic effects.

Thomas J. Talley

I was obviously born to draw better than most people, just as the widow Berman and Paul Slazinger were obviously born to tell stories better than most people can. Other people are obviously born to sing and dance or explain the stars in the sky or do magic tricks or be great leaders or athletes, and so on.

I think that could go back to the time when people had to live in small groups of relatives—maybe fifty or a hundred people at the most. And evolution or God or whatever arranged things genetically, to keep the little families going, to cheer them up, so that they could all have somebody to tell stories around the campfire at night, and somebody else to paint pictures on the walls of the caves, and somebody else who wasn't afraid of anything and so on.

That's what I think. And of course a scheme like that doesn't make sense anymore, because simply moderate giftedness has been made worthless by the printing press and radio and television and satellites and all that. A moderately gifted person who would have been a community treasure a thousand years ago has to give up, has to go into some other line of work, since modern communications put him or her into daily competition with nothing but world's champions.

The entire planet can get along nicely now with maybe a dozen champion performers in each area of human giftedness. A moderately gifted person has to keep his or her gifts all bottled up until, in a manner of speaking, he or she gets drunk at a wedding and tap-dances on the coffee table like Fred Astaire or Ginger Rogers. We have a name for him or her. We call him or her an "exhibitionist."

How do we reward such an exhibitionist? We say to him or her the next morning. "Wow! Were you ever *drunk* last night!"

Kurt Vonnegut

A ND Sunday after Sunday, we nourish a hope, faint and often unfulfilled, that our worship will take us to places of beauty and meaning we do not normally inhabit, places we have helped to create, places we will return from, refreshed and whole. "Where there is no vision," Proverbs reminds us, "the people perish" (29:18). We come to this setting to hear the sacred story and pray the great prayer with sisters and brothers, hoping to feel enlarged, expansive, full of praise, better than we are, knowing this is the way God sees us in Christ Jesus.

We cannot be trained to listen creatively, respond enthusiastically, offer warmhearted peace greetings or form images that will delight and challenge throughout the week, any more than a child can be trained to express exhilaration at finding a beautifully wrapped package under the Christmas tree, only to learn that it conceals socks and underwear. The utilitarian has little interest for a child and no place in the liturgy. The gifts that planners and ministers provide for us, their co-worshipers, must dazzle in their splendor. These persons are artists, who will have the highest respect for the art forms they render. Gifts of like quality will be given by us in return. We will act symbolically and ritually because that will be the only appropriate response.

Virginia Sloyan

MINISTERS must not clericalize the liturgy. The liturgy belongs to no one but the church, Christ's body, which is both subject and agent of every liturgical act. Since every liturgical act is an ecclesial act, liturgical ministers of whatever order are servants of this act inasmuch as they are servants of the ecclesial assembly. They must, moreover, not only be so but appear to be so.

Aidan Kavanagh

WHEN you are entertaining, try not to feel that something unusual is expected of you as a hostess. It isn't. Just be yourself. Even eminent and distinguished persons are only human. Like the rest of us, they shrink from ostentation; and nothing is more disconcerting to guests than the impression that their coming is causing a household commotion. Confine all noticeable efforts for their comfort and refreshment to the period that precedes their arrival. Satisfy yourself that you have anticipated every possible emergency—the howling child, the last-minute search for cuff links, your husband's exuberance, your helper's ineptness, your own qualms. Then relax and enjoy your guests.

If, at the last minute, something does happen to upset your well-laid plans, rise to the occasion. The mishap may be the making of your party. Capitalize on it, but not too heavily. Remember that in Roman times the poet Horace observed, "A host is like a general: It takes a mishap to reveal genius."

Irma S. Rombauer and
Marion Rombauer
Becker

SERIOUSNESS and earnestness about symbols has nothing to do with somberness or lugubriousness. Liturgy is festivity and fantasy and play. Play is to be taken seriously but not somberly. The Christian who would serve liturgical renewal and make public worship serve its purpose must learn how to play—against all of his capitalist and rationalist instincts. This is not as easy as it sounds, and its difficulty accounts for the fact that many priests and liturgical leaders who are trying to be progressive and helpful are really neither. Carelessness is not the same as play. Sloppiness is not the same as festivity. The inability to appreciate and value real things is not the same as fantasy.

When we talk about cultivating some style in celebration, we are not talking about false fronts or phoniness. We are trying to face a fundamental fact: The intimacy and informality of manner appropriate in a group of six people is as phony as a "marbleized" altar in a group of 50 or 500. Yet many of us who are leading liturgical celebrations seem to feel that there is something unreal or unauthentic about working on a discipline of style in the speech, gesture, bearing, clothing, etc., of the larger celebration. All we can think of is the old "pulpit tone," the sacred alias that presiding clergy used to assume whenever they were functioning as such. We don't want *that* at all . . . ever. But boorishness is not the only alternative to that. A patently unreal "intimacy" is not the only alternative to that. Phoniness in the other direction—pretending that every relationship in the liturgical assembly is primary and close—is just as repulsive as the pulpit tone of old.

Robert W. Hovda

S AINT Benedict begins the prologue to his *Rule* with an exhortation to the aspiring monastic: "Listen carefully . . . attend . . . with the ear of your heart." The admonition sets the theme for reflection on liturgical spirituality. We learn by heart the things we must do together in the liturgical assembly. We learn by heart in order to take to heart the saving mystery we celebrate. But learning by heart, listening with the ear of the heart, and taking to heart the mystery of Christ are the work of a lifetime, not a lesson to be mastered in a short course or a single day's participation.

Mary Collins

COMMUNITIES that have gone through periods of change and innovation become subject to boredom. In a stable ancient system, boredom is not a significant subjective dimension of experience. Monotony and repetition are characteristic of many parts of life, but these do not become sources of conscious discomfort until novelty and entertainment are built up as positive experience. . . .

In villages the world over, repetitive rituals draw their value from the fact that they are reliable reaffirmations, bringing people together within the daily round. . . . [If a] tradition is not woven into a complex interlocking web of associations [it] has a curious flat quality, like words spoken in a room where there are no echoes.

Mary Catherine
Bateson

RITUAL is a system of symbols rather than of mere signs. Symbols, being roomy, allow many different people to put them on, so to speak, in different ways. Signs do not. Signs are unambiguous because they exist to give precise information. Symbols coax one into a swamp of meaning and require one to frolic in it.

Aidan Kavanagh

SHE began with a Bach prelude and fugue. The prelude was as gaily iridescent as a prism in a morning room. The first voice of the fugue, an announcement pure and solitary, was repeated intermingling with a second voice, and again repeated with an elaborated frame, the multiple music, horizontal and serene, flowed with unhurried majesty. The principal melody was woven with two other voices, embellished with countless ingenuities—now dominant, again submerged, it had the sublimity of a single thing that does not fear surrender to the whole. Toward the end, the density of the material gathered for the last enriched insistence on the dominant first motif and with a chorded final statement the fugue ended.

Carson McCullers

Rᴇɢᴜʟᴀʀɪᴛʏ is beautiful.

There is great beauty in harmony.

Order is the creation of beauty. It is heaven's first law, and the protection of souls.

Love of Beauty has a wider field of action in association with Moral Force.

Beauty rests on utility.

All beauty that has not a foundation in use, soon grows distasteful, and needs continual replacement with something new.

That which has in itself the highest use possesses the greatest beauty.

Shaker Declarations

Hᴀᴠᴇ nothing in your houses that you do not know to be useful, or believe to be beautiful . . . accumulation of useless things not only are beautiful things kept out, but the very sense of beauty is perpetually dulled and ground away!

William Morris
Nineteenth century

A religious ritual is an agreed pattern of ceremonial movements, sounds, and verbal formulas, creating a framework within which corporate religious action can take place. If human worship is to be other than a series of solitary undertakings, some such device is plainly essential to it. We cannot do things together without some general agreement as to what is going to be done; and some willing subordination to accepted routine. Ritual, like drill, is therefore primarily justified by necessity. . . .

As we must abandon ourselves to the dance, lose ourselves in it, in order to dance well and "learn by dancing that which is done"; so with the religious rite. We can never understand it without taking part in it: moving with its movement, and yielding to its suggestions. In genuine ritual . . . the tune counts for a great deal more than the words. Moving and speaking to a measure and rhythm, the more deeply impressive because familiar and loved, we not only catch enthusiasm, but are able to carry on when enthusiasm fails. Social action reinforces our unstable fervor. Giving ourselves with humility to the common worship, we find that this common worship can rouse our sluggish instinct for holiness, support and enlighten our souls. Nor must we be too quick in assuming that improvement in the ritual of worship always consists in the triumph of words over tune; for we are concerned with an action and an experience which transcend the logical levels of the mind, and demand an artistic rather than an intellectual form of expression.

Evelyn Underhill

THESE forms are free. Few of them are commanded. Yet despite this freedom, from its very beginning the church has been pleased to select certain forms. A holy variety of singing and praying has grown up and a lovely pattern of approach to and withdrawal from the Lord of lords has been established. Just as the stars revolve around the sun, so does the congregation in its services, full of loveliness and dignity, revolve around its Lord. In holy, childlike innocence which only a child's innocent heart understands properly, the multitude of redeemed, sanctified children of God dances in worship around the universal Father and the Lamb, and the Spirit of the Lord of lords guides their steps.

Wilhelm Loehe

A high school stage play is more polished than this service we have been rehearsing since the year one. In two thousand years, we have not worked out the kinks. We positively glorify them. Week after week we witness the same miracle: that God is so mighty he can stifle his own laughter. Week after week, we witness the same miracle: that God, for reasons unfathomable, refrains from blowing our dancing bear act to smithereens. Week after week Christ washes the disciples' dirty feet, handles their very toes, and repeats, It is all right—believe it or not— to be people.

Annie Dillard   Who can believe it?

LITURGICAL celebration traditionally has been one "place," one free space in life's continuum, in which the patterns and roles and systems of daily life are humbled and reduced to size.

A liturgy of faith could not do otherwise. To celebrate in relation to God and the transcendent is inevitably to bring down the gods of daily life: power, money, status, color, sex, class, office, etc. Being a human social act, liturgy has its own structure, its own offices, and all—naturally. But in relation to the daily lives of people, it stands off, so to speak, offering the perspective of creatureliness to the powers that tend to overwhelm.

So everyone is bowed to in the liturgy, everyone is incensed, everyone is doused with water, everyone is levelled indiscriminately. Before God, and in this sacred moment consciously, the status, the class, the role, the part we play in daily life become as nothing. We can make fun of everything, of all that has confined us and restricted our freedom and made us different—vastly different—from one another.   Robert W. Hovda

IN liturgy as in life, the stakes are high.   Nathan Mitchell

POPULAR religiosity responds to the affective side of religion and goes to the very heart of the individual and community. It is for this reason that popular religious customs and practices have endured some four hundred years in the Hispanic community and have been transported into new lands and cultures. They seem to give our lives a certain consistency and keep us on a steady course. They are the living symbols that touch us deeply. Therefore, what has been transplanted from across the border into this act of worship is not peripheral, but is the very heart of our people, and we seek to offer this heartful act of worship to others.

Implicit in this approach is the challenge to the individual-istic values and tendencies of our society. Bishop Ricardo Ramirez calls this the "prophetic role" of Hispanic worship, in which customs of the dominant culture are questioned, given priorities are reevaluated, and absolutes are redefined. Worship is the act which highlights the criteria for evaluat-ing society's influences, and which provides our people with the basis for incorporating other values into our lives.

Arturo Peréz

THE clichés of student culture are no more inherently pro-found than the clichés of any other group. Left-wing poli-tics can be as much an escape from reality as compulsive money-making. There is the danger, then, of simply switch-ing from one style of culture religion to another. To the extent that the traditional religious symbols operated to call into question and not simply to validate the contemporary cultural materials in the service, the danger was avoided.

Robert Bellah

GREAT artists are not transcribers of the scheme of things; they are its rivals.

André Malraux

IT's only modern vanity which supposes that everything can be known or that only what is knowable has a claim upon our interest. The artist and the priest know that there are mysteries beyond anything that can be done with words, sounds or forms. If we want to live without this sense of mystery, we can of course, but we should be very suspicious of the feeling that everything coheres and that the arts, like everything else, fit comfortably into our lives.

Denis Donoghue

G OD may be of no concern to us, but we are of much concern to God. The only way to discover this is the ultimate way, the way of worship. For worship is a way of living, a way of seeing the world in the light of God. To worship is to rise to a higher level of existence, to see the world from the point of view of God. In worship we discover that the ultimate way is not to have a symbol but *to be a symbol,* to stand for the divine.

Abraham Joshua Heschel

T HE world and its history are the terrible and sublime liturgy, breathing of death and sacrifice, which God celebrates and causes to be celebrated in and through human history in its freedom, this being something which God in turn sustains in grace by sovereign disposition. In the entire length and breadth of this immense history of birth and death, complete superficiality, folly, inadequacy and hatred (all of which "crucify") on the one hand, and silent submission, responsibility even to death in dying and in joyfulness, in attaining the heights and plumbing the depths, on the other, the true liturgy of the world is present—present in such a way that the liturgy which the Son has brought to its absolute fullness on his cross belongs intrinsically to it, emerges from it, i.e., from the ultimate source of the grace of the world, and constitutes the supreme point of *this* liturgy from which all else draws its life, because everything else is always dependent upon the supreme point as upon its goal and at the same time sustained by it. This liturgy of the world is as it were veiled to the darkened eyes and the dulled heart which fails to understand its own true nature. This liturgy, therefore must, if the individual is really to share in the celebration of it in all freedom and self-commitment even to death, be interpreted, "reflected upon" in its ultimate depths in the celebration of that which we are accustomed to call liturgy in the more usual sense.

Karl Rahner

As the most basic and fundamental liturgy, this liturgy of the world provides the original objective content for our notion of liturgy. When we think of liturgy, we should think first and foremost of the liturgy of the world. Worship is not primarily what happens when we gather together to celebrate the eucharist; it is primarily what happens when we cooperate together with God in history. Liturgy is not originally the praise we give to God when we pray; it is what happens when we freely immerse ourselves in the abiding, absolute mystery during the great and small moments of life. The liturgy is most basically that pattern of God's reconciling self-communication evoking our thankful self-surrender, which is woven inextricably through our history. Worship is fundamentally the quiet, unobtrusive exchange of self-gifts between the absolute mystery and the human community. Here we find the essential experience of God's free self-communication to us and our free self-donation to God. This liturgy, which takes place throughout the world and human history, is the original liturgy. The liturgy of the church is one way in which the liturgy of the world is revealed and celebrated.

Michael Skelley

To landscape the imagination; to feed and free it by the power-laden symbols of life and death, failure and finitude, absence and plenty, debt and grandeur: that is liturgy's redeeming work in and for the life of the world. *Liturgy* is what underwrites the social contract — and it is ultimately what shapes and conditions all love and enjoyment in our world.

Nathan Mitchell

If then, praise and thanksgiving necessarily flow from the fact that the gift has in reality been given, and hence are evoked in an inward way by "secular worship," the relationship between the church's liturgy and secular worship will reflect this. The *berākhāh*—the praise of God from which the eucharist first took its structure—or the church's present liturgy will, of course, be without value if the reality which sustains it, our relationship of service to our brothers and sisters in the world, is not in fact there; for this secular worship in its *deepest dimension,* as the gift of grace, is what is expressed and acknowledged in prayer and the liturgy within the intersubjective sphere of those who share the faith. Without secular worship, prayer and the church's liturgy, our speaking of and to God become simply an ideological supra-structure without roots in the realities of life, and hence artificial. Our praise of God's majesty and of God's love for us—"God is my song"—belongs essentially to the total structure of our love of God which realizes itself in love and concern for our brothers and sisters. . . .

If the church's liturgy were reduced to what presupposes and at the same time gives rise to liturgy—that is "secular worship," in which God is only implicitly experienced in secular life, or brought down to the level of a pleasant little chat consisting of "good morning" and "have a nice weekend"—then this liturgy would be a serious misconception not only of the "spiritual sacrifice" implied by our being in the world in the light of community with God but also of the profoundly human dimension which is expressed in the thankful celebration of all that gives our lives meaning and makes them worth living. And this is certainly no trivial commonplace, but the "seriousness of divine love," made historically tangible among us in Jesus' human love of God which had the form of a radical love of human-beings "to the end."

Edward Schillebeeckx

R ECONCILIATION in the New Testament sense does not consist in plea bargaining with God. Nor does it have anything to do with amassing virtue so that God will somehow be forced, in justice, to bestow grace and salvation. If the radical meaning of repentance is "recognition and response," then the meaning of reconciliation is *obedience* and *surrender.* Being obedient to the word of the gospel does not mean the perfect fulfilling of laws, regulations and prescriptions. It means, instead, letting go, giving up our pretentious claims to goodness and holiness, surrendering to the power of God's love that burns even our virtues away.

It is this subversive love of God that the sacrament of reconciliation intends to celebrate. The sacrament is important not because it *removes* something (sin, guilt, punishment), but because it *proclaims* something: that God reconciles us precisely as enemies, precisely as sinners (cf. Romans 5:10). While one would not want to repudiate the psychological benefits of confession (the alleviation of anxiety through the disclosure of failure and guilt to another person), such benefits are not the primary purpose of reconciliation as a sacramental celebration of the church's faith. The fundamental intention of the sacrament is not the excavation of the human psyche nor even the therapeutic release of anxiety. The sacrament of reconciliation is a proclamation of faith; it is a public moment of thanksgiving and praise when the church confesses its faith in the God whose predictable love appears in unpredictable places.

Like the stories of Jesus and like the cross itself, the sacrament of reconciliation is a parable. Its message is provocative, subversive, unexpected; it overturns all human judgments about virtue and vice, sinners and saints. As a parable the sacrament of reconciliation continues the proclamation of the kingdom begun in the ministry of Jesus. Jesus announced a kingdom where the great are small, the rich are poor, the lepers are clean, the prostitutes are virtuous, the sinners sit down at table with God, and the mighty cedars of Lebanon are scrubby mustard plants. This kingdom, Jesus suggested, defies all human expectations about how God works in the world. To the powerful, God's reign will appear shabby, incompetent and absurd; to the powerless, it will appear awesome, royal and overwhelming. To *all*, God's reign will be puzzling, controversial and even annoying. Predictions about it are useless—it comes like a thief in the night; theologies about it are futile—its secret is revealed to the unlearned.

The sacrament of reconciliation is a parable of this reign or kingdom of God. Far from being an occasion of private surgery where sins are aborted in secret, reconciliation publicly announces the central paradox of Christian faith: the fact that the words "God," "love" and "sinner" must be put together in the same sentence.

Nathan Mitchell

Whenyou have partaken of this sacrament, therefore, or desire to partake of it, you must in turn share the misfortunes of the fellowship, as has been said. But what are these? Christ in heaven and the angels, together with the saints, have no misfortunes, except when injury is done to the truth and to the word of God. Indeed, as we have said, every bane and blessing of all the saints on earth affects them. Here your heart must go out in love and learn that this is a sacrament of love. As love and support are given you, you in turn must render love and support to Christ in his needy ones. You must feel with sorrow all the dishonor done to Christ in his holy word, all the misery of Christendom, all the unjust suffering of the innocent, with which the world is everywhere filled to overflowing. You must fight, work, pray, and—if you cannot do more—have heartfelt sympathy.

Martin Luther
Sixteenth century

Forcenturies, the liturgy, actively celebrated, has been the most important form of pastoral care.

Joseph Jungmann

Thedoom-sayers who complain that Roman Catholic worship has lost its mystery have forgotten, perhaps, that symbols are not tidy museum exhibits but messy transactions that involve the fundamental stuff of human existence: earth, air, fire, water; eggs, seed, fluid and meat; marriage, sex, birth, death. The merit of our recent reforms lies precisely in a re-ordering of the relationship between ritual symbols and human life. By "shortening the distance" between liturgical rites and the ordinary rituals of daily living (through use of the vernacular, for example), a more powerful confrontation between the two can occur. In a word, the reforms move us closer to the raw nerve-center of Christian symbols. We are invited to inch our way toward the edge of the raft, without the benefit of comforting buffers provided by such things as a dead language (such languages are easy to control and manipulate), silent prayers (which are readily ignored or replaced by our own pieties), and cushiony "background" music. Shortening the distance between ourselves and our ritual symbols allows those symbols to sift, critique, shape and judge the quality of our lives. In the reformed rites we find fewer hiding places.

Nathan Mitchell

L ITURGY rather than doctrine or theology will become the place where the whole community of believers will attempt to give expression to its experience of saving relationships. . . .

Intellectually, we may know there is room enough in the body of Christ for every person and that there is wisdom in ordering spiritual gifts and ministries. Yet the eucharistic assembly is the ritual territory in which this struggle for spiritual identity and relational significance is being played out. How we are related to one another and to God in Christ and the Spirit, how we all participate in his death for the life of the world is a crucial spiritual issue for committed Christians in this age of church and liturgical reform and renewal. The eucharistic assembly will one day be the place where a transformed Catholic consciousness will present itself, just as it is now the embodiment of our confusion, our resentment, our passivity, and whatever hope, enthusiasm, and new insight the baptized people of God may have.

Mary Collins

F OR to my mind the principal problem, indeed crisis, facing liturgy in this country is that of credibility. Despite all the revision and reform (and sometimes perhaps because of it), a hiatus amounting in many cases to a chasm of Grand Canyon proportions has opened up between language and experience, between description and reality, between ideology and fact. Thus: "families" whose members know nothing of each other, "communities" which are nothing of the sort, "songs" which are recited, "acclamations" which are muttered by one voice, baptisms where people are "bathed" and "buried" in Christ under 10ml of water and "welcomed into a community" which has not bothered to turn up or even been informed of the event, "meals" at which no one drinks and where "sharing one bread" means consumption of 500 individual breads, "gifts of the people" which are not theirs and which they do not give, "celebrations" which are the joyless and perfunctory discharge of an obligation. The list is depressing and almost infinitely extensible. It is questionable how long the liturgy can endure this corrupting disease without being irretrievably weakened. What is increasingly clear is that the condition can no longer, if it ever could, be rectified simply by adjustments to the words, actions and explanations of the liturgy. It is already beginning to look as if far too much attention and energy have been devoted to the words, rubrics and translations of the liturgy, which have been examined, revised, criticized and fought over almost in a vacuum of narcissistic introversion. Joseph Gelineau ends his recent book on the future of the liturgy wondering "if the liturgy today is not more preoccupied with itself than with the Kingdom it proclaims." Reforms and revisions we have had in plenty, but liturgical *renewal* will never be achieved until our texts, rites and affirmations are translated not into this or that sort of English but into reality in the lived experience of the people; and they will rarely be experienced as real until the congregations celebrating them are genuine communities of faith, witness and action.

Christopher J. Walsh

THE Sacred Council has several aims in view: it desires to impart an ever increasing vigor to the Christian life of the faithful; to adapt more suitably to the needs of our own times those institutions that are subject to change; to foster whatever can promote union among all who believe in Christ; to strengthen whatever can help to call the whole of humanity into the household of the church. The Council therefore sees particularly cogent reasons for undertaking the reform and promotion of the liturgy.

For the liturgy, "making the work of our redemption a present actuality," most of all in the divine sacrifice of the eucharist, is the outstanding means whereby the faithful may express in their lives and manifest to others the mystery of Christ and the real nature of the true church. It is of the essence of the church to be both human and divine, visible yet endowed with invisible resources, eager to act yet intent on contemplation, present in this world yet not at home in it; and the church is all these things in such wise that in it the human is directed and subordinated to the divine, the visible likewise to the invisible, action to contemplation, and this present world to that city yet to come which we seek. While the liturgy daily builds up those who are within into a holy temple of the Lord, into a dwelling place for God in the Spirit, to the mature measure of the fullness of Christ, at the same time it marvelously strengthens their power to preach Christ and thus shows forth the church to those who are outside as a sign lifted up among the nations, under which the scattered children of God may be gathered together, until there is one sheepfold and one shepherd. . . .

The liturgy is the summit toward which the activity of the church is directed; at the same time it is the fount from which all the church's power flows. For the aim and object of apostolic works is that all who are made children of God by faith and baptism should come together to praise God in the midst of the church, to take part in the sacrifice, and to eat the Lord's Supper. . . .

The church earnestly desires that all the faithful be led to that full, conscious, and active participation in liturgical celebrations called for by the very nature of the liturgy. Such participation by the Christian people as "a chosen race, a royal priesthood, a holy nation, God's own people" (1 Peter 2:9, see 2:4–5) is their right and duty by reason of their baptism.

In the reform and promotion of the liturgy, this full and active participation by all the people is the aim to be considered before all else. For it is the primary and indispensable source from which the faithful are to derive the true Christian spirit and therefore pastors must zealously strive in all their pastoral work to achieve such participation by means of the necessary instruction.

Yet it would be futile to entertain any hopes of realizing this unless, in the first place, the pastors themselves become thoroughly imbued with the spirit and power of the liturgy and make themselves its teachers. . . .

Zeal for the promotion and restoration of the liturgy is rightly held to be a sign of the providential dispositions of God in our time, a movement of the Holy Spirit in the church. Today it is a distinguishing mark of the church's life, indeed of the whole tenor of contemporary religious thought and action.   Vatican Council II

FROM the Greek λειτουργία, "action of the people"; the term used in the Septuagint for worship. Liturgy is the official service of God offered by the mystical body of Jesus Christ, head and members (thus *Mediator Dei*, Pius XII's encyclical on the liturgy, 1947). According to the Epistle to the Hebrews Jesus Christ as high priest is a λειτουργός. In the book of Revelation adoration is offered to God and the Lamb with solemn ceremonies. The NT Epistles include hymns that may have been sung at services but no instructions for the latter. During the first few centuries religious services and the prayers used in them were certainly improvised according to the basic pattern of a meal commemorative of Christ's death, and a service of readings and prayers, with a sermon and a confession of faith; the earliest traditional formulae are only meant to be examples; such formulae were first made obligatory about 600 CE at Rome. Only with the progress of theological reflexion did the official text harden into a fixed form, on order that none of its numerous elements should be forgotten: Christ's office as mediator, dramatic symbolism (either of Christ's life or of the heavenly liturgy), anamnesis of the Lord's death linked with a commemoration of the saints, etc. The final step in this process was the preservation of purely ecclesiastical languages (that is "dead" languages). A genuine liturgical revival should not be content to restore primitive forms but ought to discover the liturgical forms for the celebration of the eucharist and the hearing of the word of God that are appropriate *today,* just as the early church chose forms appropriate to its own time. But this is impossible without exact appreciation and theological analysis of the present. In a fundamental document, the Constitution on the Liturgy of Vatican II, the church has laid down broad principles the application of which in pastoral practice must be one of the major tasks of our generation and the effects of which in the restoration of Catholic life are incalculable, in a recovery from within of the sense of the church as a worshiping community.

Karl Rahner,
Herbert Vorgrimler

UNFORTUNATELY the cardinal ran on longer than his allotted ten minutes, refusing to be interrupted by the President, Cardinal Alfrink, who politely interposed: "Excuse me, Eminence, but you have already spoken more than fifteen minutes." The Secretary General, Archbishop Felici, thereupon conferred with Cardinal Alfrink, and Ottaviani was forced to stop; the microphone was then turned over to the next speaker. The Council fathers expressed their displeasure with the tenor of this speech by applauding Cardinal Alfrink's action. It was the unmistakable sign of the general feeling of the assembly, rather than the intervention of Alfrink, which seems to have caused Ottaviani to feel insulted and to remain away for almost two weeks.

Xavier Rynne

A new inspiration springs forth with every time, with every age, with every place. In the song of the church there is always one more measure, one more note, one more verse, more lyrics, and above all, more deeds to perform, deeds that build the temple of the kingdom of God.

Ricardo Ramirez

Liturgical prayer would soon become powerless were the faithful not to take a real share in it, or at least not to associate themselves to it in heart. It can heal and save the world, but only on the condition that it be understood. Be wise, then, ye children of the Catholic church, and obtain that largeness of heart which will make you pray the prayer of your mother. Come and by your share in it fill up that harmony which is so sweet to the ear of God. Where would you obtain the spirit of prayer if not at its natural source? Let us remind you of the exhortation of the apostle to the first Christians: "Let the peace of Christ rejoice in your hearts; let the word of Christ dwell in you abundantly, in all wisdom; teaching and admonishing one another, in psalms, hymns, and spiritual canticles, singing in grace in your hearts to God" (Colossians 3:15–16).

For a long time, a remedy has been devised for an evil which was only vaguely felt. The spirit of prayer, and even prayer itself, has been sought for in methods and prayer books, which contain, it is true, laudable, yea, pious thoughts, but after all only human thoughts. Such nourishment cannot satisfy the soul, for it does not initiate into the prayer of the church. Instead of uniting the soul with the prayer of the church it isolates. Of this kind are so many of those collections of prayers and reflections, which have been published under different titles during the last 200 years, and by which it was intended to edify the faithful, and suggest to them, either for hearing Mass, or going to the sacraments, or keeping the feasts of the church, certain more or less commonplace considerations and acts, always drawn up according to the manner of thought and sentiment peculiar to the author of each book. Each manual had consequently its own way of treating these important subjects. To Christians already formed to piety, such books as these would, indeed, serve a purpose, especially as nothing better was offered to them; but they had not influence sufficient to inspire with the spirit of prayer such as had not otherwise received it.

It may perhaps be objected that, were all practical books of Christian piety to be reduced to mere explanations of the liturgy, we should run the risk of impoverishing, and even destroying, by excessive formalities, the spirit of prayer and contemplation, which is such a precious gift of the Holy Ghost to the church of God. To this we answer that by asserting the immense superiority of liturgical over individual prayer, we do not say that individual methods should be suppressed; we would only wish them to be kept in their proper place.

Prosper Gueranger
Nineteenth century

NOW it would be disastrous if the liturgical renewal were to rely on the replacement of one kind of constraint by the other. Renewal means, on the contrary, the replacement of constraint by the openness of simple and joyous participation. Those who have emotional conflicts — and after all, who doesn't? — will do best if they can realize that this openness is practically the only thing that can ease their anxieties in this particular sphere. It will help them, by humility, grace, self-forgetfulness and trust to approach the Lord who will heal them in the relaxed and expanded atmosphere of love which is ideally that of liturgical worship.

Thomas Merton

MANY of us have not understood how past and present are united. Too frequently we have tended to see the developments in the sacred liturgy as the work of faddists and dreamers; we have failed to realize that the church has been leading us to a new understanding over a long period. Now we have arrived at the time of decision. The church in solemn proclamation has placed the renewal of sacred worship at the very heart of the church's life and the people's need. The guiding principles of reform and restoration have been announced; they are eminently pastoral. They lie at the heart of the vocation of every Christian, and in a special way at the heart of every priest. No one can be excused now if they fail to make the study and effort for success....

See in all the changes which have been decreed and which will affect your lives, not new burdens, but matchless opportunities to express your own Christian identity, as a people made holy to the Lord. Give yourselves cheerfully, willingly, and unselfishly to those periods of instruction and practice which are required so that the public worship of the church may be authentically and fully expressed in your own parish.   Richard Cushing

THE revisions may appear complex to the priest celebrant or to the ministers and servers, who have understandably formed routines and habits. But far from creating complexity for the faithful, they may at last show that the Mass is not a series of prayers recited by the priest, but a balanced composite of song by the people, lessons proclaimed by a reader, prayers led by the priest, culminating in the eucharistic prayer. . . .

No one should seek an end to necessary and fundamental rubrical or ceremonial directions — as no one should be so arrogant as to create their own liturgy. But we should welcome the freedom and flexibility built into the liturgical reform, so that the celebration in the Christian community may become a living and real thing, the sign of genuine prayer and faith.   Frederick R. McManus

EVERYWHERE I go, I find believers, or people who want to find a way to believe, saying that they would like somebody to "explain the Mass" to them. In the deepest sense, it really cannot be explained, if it really is the Mass. If it really is the body and blood of the Messiah, then there is always more to it than we shall find within the limits of our own little time and place in this world. But there is another sense in which explanation can and must be given. The Mass must unfold for people in a way that touches their hearts and their lives. Otherwise, it will indeed be without meaning for them. All too often, explanations are given that are not explanations at all, because they are not faithful to the way people actually live and believe and experience the Mass today. . . .

The ancient ritual of the Mass has recently undergone reform. Often enough, that reform has been implemented halfheartedly or ineptly. Where this happens, the Mass is robbed of much of its power, beauty and possibility. And so, serious commentary cannot simply gloss over the sad experience of ignorant or uncaring use of our ceremonies. The official Mass book of the church, *The Roman Missal,* insists in its very first chapter that the Mass is the action of the entire church. Thus responsibility for its decent celebration does not rest solely with the clergy. It is the right and the duty of the laity to protest ignorant or careless use of our ceremonies. In a word, responsible commentary demands that we acknowledge that doubt is part of believing, that dissent and disagreement is part of adult belonging, and that, often enough, more than bread is broken at our altars.

Ralph A. Keifer

THE Sunday liturgy is not the church assembled to address itself. The liturgy thus does not cater to the assembly. It summons the assembly to enact itself publicly for the life of the world. Nor does this take place as a dialogue with the world, often a partner whose uninterested absence reduces the dialogue to an ecclesiastical monologue. The liturgy presumes that the world is always present in the summoned assembly, which although not of "this world" lives deep in its midst as the corporate agent, under God in Christ, of its salvation. In this view, the liturgical assembly *is* the world being renovated according to the divine pleasure—not as patient being passively worked upon but as active agent faithfully cooperating in its own rehabilitation. What one witnesses in the liturgy is the world being done as the world's Creator and Redeemer will the world to be done. The liturgy does the world and does it as its very center, for it is here that the world's malaise and its cure well up together, inextricably entwined.

Aidan Kavanagh

Unless Christian commitment to works of justice is integrated into the deepest level of Christian self-understanding through significant eucharistic renewal, the dreary alternative will be a new age of Catholic moralizing, only now generating guilt over social as well as sexual sin. Maturity of faith grounded in an integrated understanding of the mystery of Christ is necessary to sustain the new ecclesial commitment to justice. "Can you drink the cup I shall drink or be baptized in the same bath of pain as I?" (Mark 10:38) The liturgical posing of the challenge and the faith-filled response of the church gathered for public worship is at the heart of the church's spiritual growth in this regard.

We are going to start on an unexplored path.... We shall innovate, do what our ancestors and forbears could not or dared not do.... Here is one solution we have not tried ... commitment to action on behalf of justice and participation in the transformation of the world based on our eucharistic communion in the blood of Christ.

Mary Collins

THE greatest gift which we are asked to accept is the gift of living our lives reverently. We are assured that Jesus came not that we may have more "prayers," or more reading of the scriptures, or more pious devotions, or more of anything, but only "that (we) may live life and have it more abundantly."

Joseph F. Schmidt

THE paschal mystery is not a cold and lifeless representation of the events of the past, or a simple and bare record of a former age. It is rather Christ himself who is ever living in his church. Here he continues that journey of immense mercy which he began in his mortal life . . . with the design of bringing people to know his mysteries and in a way live by them. These mysteries are ever present and active.

Mediator Dei

EACH church gathers regularly to praise and thank God, to remember and make present God's great deeds, to offer common prayer, to realize and celebrate the kingdom of peace and justice. That action of the Christian assembly is liturgy.

Environment and Art in Catholic Worship

Endnotes

I cannot achieve: From *The Times Are Never So Bad* by Andre Dubus. Published by David R. Godine Publisher, Inc., Boston, 1983. Used with permission.

There is a: From "Vesting of Liturgical Ministers" in *Worship*, March 1980. Reprinted by permission of St. John's Abbey, Collegeville, Minnesota.

Creation often: From *Prose Pieces: Essays and Stories*. Published by Random House, Inc., New York, 1988.

It is either: Reprinted with permission of Scribner's, an imprint of Simon & Schuster from *Man's Quest for God* by Abraham Joshua Heschel. Copyright © 1954, Abraham Joshua Heschel; copyright renewed © 1982, Hannah Susannah Heschel and Sylvia Heschel.

To be a person: From *Prayer as a Political Problem* by Jean Danielous. Reprinted by permission of Sheed & Ward, Inc., New York.

I undressed: From *Report to Greco* by Nikos Kazantzakis, translated by P. A. Bien. Published by Simon and Schuster, New York, 1965.

During a feast: From *Beyond Conventional Christianity* translated by Kathleen England, OSU. Published by East Asian Pastoral Institute, Manila, 1974.

When the liturgy: From *The Splendour of the Liturgy* by Maruize Zundel. Reprinted by permission of Sheed & Ward, Inc., New York.

The Ascension: From *Theological Investigations, vol. 7.* Reprinted by permission of the Crossroad Publishing Company.

But when Jesus: From *Liturgy and Social Justice* edited by Mark Searle. Copyright © 1980, The Order of St. Benedict. Reprinted with permission of The Liturgical Press.

To name a thing: From *For the Life of the World: Sacraments and Orthodoxy* by Alexander Schmemann. Copyright © 1963, 1970, 1971, 1973, Alexander Schmemann. Reprinted by permission of St. Vladimir's Seminary Press, Crestwood, New York.

To the total: From *The Divine Milieu* by Pierre Teilhard de Chardin. Copyright © 1957, Editions du Seuil, Paris; English translation copyright © 1960, Wm. Collins Sons & Co., London, and Harper & Row., Publishers, Inc., New York. Renewed © 1988, Harper & Row Publishers, Inc. Reprinted by permission of HarperCollins Publishers, Inc.

To worship: From *Worship and Secular Man* by Raimundo Panikkar. Published by Orbis Books, Maryknoll, New York, 1973.

The Christian hope: From *Worship* by Evelyn Underhill. Copyright © 1936, Harper & Row Publishers, Inc. Copyright renewed. Reprinted by permission of HarperCollins Publishers, Inc.

Look, the trees: From *New and Selected Poems* by Mary Oliver. Copyright © 1992, Mary Oliver. Reprinted with permission of Beacon Press, Boston.

City, when: From *Selected Poems of Thomas Merton.* Copyright © 1963, The Abbey of Gethsemani, Inc. Reprinted by pemission of New Directions Publishing Corporation, New York.

You enter into: Reprinted from *Meditations with (10) Teresa of Avila* by Camille Campbell. Copyright © 1985, Bear & Co., Inc., P.O. Box 2860, Santa Fe NM 87504.

For baptism: From *Luther's Works,* vol. 35 in *Word and Sacrament,* edited by E. Theodore Bachmann. Published by Concordia Publishing House and Muhlenberg Press, Philadelphia, 1960.

There is the story: From *The Worship of the Church: A Companion to Liturgical Studies* by William J. O'Shea. Published by The Newman Press, New York, 1957.

Judge, every: Reprinted with the permission of Scribner's, an imprint of Simon & Schuster from *Ah, But Your Land Is Beautiful* by Alan Paton. Copyright © 1981, Alan Paton.

A meal celebrated: From *Eucharist: Symbol of Transformation* by William R. Crockett. Copyright © 1989, Pueblo Publishing Co., Inc. Reprinted by permission of The Liturgical Press, Collegeville, Minnesota.

The liturgical worship: From "Liturgy and Imagination" in *Worship*, March 1992. Reprinted by permission of St. John's Abbey, Collegeville, Minnesota.

Now we urge: Excerpt from the English translation of *The Liturgy of the Hours.* Copyright © 1974, International Committee on English in the Liturgy, Inc. All rights reserved.

When the liturgy: From *Politics and Liturgy* edited by Herman Schmidt and David Power. Published by Herder and Herder, New York, 1974.

How, then, can: From *Liturgy and Life,* a Pastoral Letter by Richard Cardinal Cushing. Reprinted with permission of the Archdiocese of Boston.

The success: From *Worship in a New Key: What the Council Teaches on the Liturgy* by Gerard S. Sloyan.

Published by Echo Books, a Division of Doubleday & Company, Inc., Garden City, New York, 1966.

The commitment: From *Our Communion, Our Peace, Our Promise, a Pastoral Letter on the Liturgy* by Joseph Cardinal Bernardin. Published by Liturgy Training Publications, 1984.

I simply: From *Dry Bones: Living Worship Guides to Good Liturgy.* Copyright The Liturgical Conference, 8750 Georgia Avenue, Suite 123, Silver Spring MD 20910-3621. All rights reserved. Used with permission.

Victor, who presided: From *Eusebius: The Ecclesiastical History,* translated by Kirsopp Lake. Published by Harvard University Press, Cambridge, Massachusetts.

As I was: From *Christianity Rediscovered.* Published by Orbis Books, Maryknoll, New York.

The primary: From *The Church and the Catholic* by Romano Guardini, translated by Ada Lane. Reprinted by permission of Sheed & Ward, Inc., New York.

(20) **True worship:** From *Worship and Spirituality* by Don E. Saliers. Published by Westminster Press, Philadelphia, 1984.

Neither the vigil: From *The Shape of Baptism: The Rite of Christian Initiation* by Aidan Kavanagh. Copyright © 1978, Pueblo Publishing Co., Inc. Reprinted by permission of The Liturgical Press, Collegeville, Minnesota.

Sacrament, that: From "What Does Liturgy Do?" in *Worship,* May 1992. Reprinted by permission of St. John's Abbey, Collegeville, Minnesota.

It is not safe: Reprinted with permission of Scribner's, an imprint of Simon & Schuster from *Man's Quest for God* by Abraham Joshua Heschel. Copyright © 1954, Abraham Joshua Heschel; copyright renewed © 1982, Hannah Susannah Heschel and Sylvia Heschel.

What do people: Reprinted from *Worshipful Preaching* by Gerard Sloyan. Copyright © 1984, Fortress Press. Used with permission of Augsburg Fortress.

They devoted: From *The Catholic Study Bible.* Published by Oxford University Press, New York, 1990.

The morning after: From *Inside, Outside* by Herman Wouk. Published by Avon Books, New York, 1985.

Imagine a building: From *Concerning the Spiritual in Art* by Wassily Kandinsky, translated by M. T. H. Sadler. Copyright © 1977, Dover Publications, Inc., New York. Used with permission.

Never before: From *The Life of Cardinal Cheverus* by J. Huen-Dubourg. Published by James Munroe and Company, Boston, 1939.

The churchwomen: From *Holy the Firm* by Annie Dillard. Copyright © 1977, Annie Dillard. Reprinted by permission of HarperCollins Publishers, Inc.

The assumption: From *The Reenchantment of Art* by Suzi Gablik. Published by Thames and Hudson, Inc., New York, 1991.

Beware, my: From *The Reenchantment of Art* by Suzi Gablik. Published by Thames and Hudson, Inc., New York, 1991.

One of our: From *The Screwtape Letters* by C. S. Lewis. Copyright © 1942, C. S. Lewis. Used with permission of HarperCollins Publishers, Ltd.

The liturgical assembly: From *On Liturgical Theology* by Aidan Kavanagh. Copyright © 1984, Pueblo Publishing Co., Inc. Reprinted by permission of The Liturgical Press, Collegeville, Minnesota.

Because of the: From *Worship: Renewal to Practice* by Mary Collins, OSB. Copyright © 1987, The Pastoral Press, Washington, D. C. Used with permission.

Liturgical prayer: From *The Place of Christ in Liturgical Prayer* by Joseph Jungmann, SJ. Published by Alba House, 1965.

The Christian faith: From *The Liturgy of the Hours in East and West* by Robert Taft, SJ. Reprinted with permission of The Liturgical Press.

The theological: "Collecting and Recollecting: The Mystery of the Gathered Church" in *Assembly,* September 1984. Reprinted with permission of Notre Dame Center for Pastoral Liturgy.

God should: Excerpt from the English translation of Documents on the Liturgy, 1963–1979: Conciliar, Papal and Curial Texts. Copyright © 1982, International Committee on English in the Liturgy, Inc. All rights reserved.

Among the symbols: From *Environment and Art in Catholic Worship,* 1978. Reprinted by permission of the United States Catholic Conference, Washington, D.C. (30)

Very good, Asherel: From *My Name Is Asher Lev* by Chaim Potok. Published by Fawcett Crest Books, New York.

If a poor man: From *Early Sources of the Liturgy* compiled and edited by Lucien Deiss, CSSP. Reprinted with permission of The Liturgical Press.

To the bath: From *Holy Things: A Liturgical Theology* by Gordon W. Lathrop. Published by Augsburg Fortress Publishers, 1993.

Even if you: From *Music in Early Christian Litera-ture,* edited by James McKinnon. Reprinted with permission of Cambridge University Press.

It is fitting: From *The Apostolic Fathers* translated by Kirsopp Lake. Published by Harvard University Press, Cambridge, Massachusetts.

What is more: From *Music in Early Christian Literature,* edited by James McKinnon. Reprinted with permission of Cambridge University Press.

In a sense: Reprinted with permission of Scribner's, an imprint of Simon & Schuster from *Man's Quest for God* by Abraham Joshua Heschel. Copyright © 1954, Abraham Joshua Heschel; copyright renewed © 1982, Hannah Susannah Heschel and Sylvia Heschel.

I am not satisfied: From *Ministry through Word and Sacrament* by Thomas C. Oden. Published by The Crossroad Publishing Company, New York, 1989.

Not long ago: From *Dakota.* Copyright © 1993, Kathleen Norris. Reprinted by permission of Ticknor & Fields/Houghton Mifflin Co. All rights reserved.

Rebbe David: From *Souls on Fire* by Elie Wiesel, translated by Marion Wiesel. Published by Summit Books, New York, 1972.

All desires: From *Music and the Experience of God* edited by Mary Collins, David Power and Mellonee Burnim. Published by T. & T. Clark Ltd., Edinburgh, 1989.

O the happiness: Excerpt from the English transla-tion of *The Liturgy of the Hours.* Copyright © 1974, International Committee on English in the Liturgy, Inc. All rights reserved.

Do but so live: From *William Law: A Serious Call to a Devout and Holy Life* edited by Paul G. Stanwood. Reprinted by permission of Paulist Press, New York.

Speaking to yourselves: From *The Art of Prayer: An Orthodox Anthology* compiled by Igumen Chariton of Valamo, translated by E. Kadloubovsky and E. M. Palmer. Reprinted by permission of Faber and Faber, Ltd.

The hand on: From *New Poems* by Pablo Neruda. English translation copyright © 1972, Ben Belitt. Used by permission of Grove/Atlantic, Inc., New York.

Learn these tunes: From *The United Methodist Hymnal.* Copyright © 1989, The United Methodist Publishing House. Used with permission.

With the: From *Music and Worship in Pagan & Christian Antiquity* by Johannes Quasten. Copyright © 1983, National Association of Pastoral Musicians, Washington, D. C. Used with permission.

When in our music: "When in our music God is glorified" by Fred Pratt Green. Words copyright © 1972, Hope Publishing Co., Carol Stream, Illinois. All rights reserved. Used with permission.

Undoubtedly: From *Theories of Modern Art: A Source Book by Artists and Critics* by Herschel B. Chipp. Published by the University of California Press, Berkeley.

Preference for: From "Spirituality of Mexican Americans" in *Worship,* May 1989. Reprinted by per-mission of St. John's Abbey, Collegeville, Minnesota.

The sublime: Excerpt from *God in Search of Man.* (40) Copyright © 1955, Abraham Joshua Heschel; renewed 1983, Sylvia Heschel. Published by per-mission of Farrar, Straus and Giroux, Inc.

While our words: From *Environment and Art in Catholic Worship,* 1978. Reprinted by permission of the United States Catholic Conference, Washington, D. C.

Liturgy happens: From *On Liturgical Theology* by Aidan Kavanagh. Copyright © 1984, Pueblo Pub-lishing Co., Inc. Reprinted by permission of The Liturgical Press, Collegeville, Minnesota.

The only really: From *The Ratzinger Report.* Published by Ignatius Press, San Francisco, 1985.

The special quality: From *The Unknown Craftsman* by Soetsu Yanagi. Published by Kodansha Inter-national, 1972.

How can I: From *Holy the Firm* by Annie Dillard. Copyright © 1977, Annie Dillard. Reprinted by per-mission of HarperCollins Publishers, Inc.

The dance: "Book" in *Assembly,* September 1981. Reprinted with permission of Notre Dame Center for Pastoral Liturgy.

The flesh: "Oil & Chrism" in *Assembly,* September 1981. Reprinted with permission of Notre Dame Center for Pastoral Liturgy.

While the congregation: From *The Divine Liturgy according to the Maronite Antiochian Rite.* Pub-lished by the Maronite Chancery Office, Detroit, Michigan, 1969.

Your questions are: From *The Art Spirit* by Robert Henri. Copyright © 1923, J. B. Lippincott Company. Renewal copyright © 1951, Violet Organ. Reprinted by permission of HarperCollins Publishers, Inc.

Thus, when: From *Abbott Suger on the Abbey Church of St. Denis* edited by Erwin Panofsky. Published by Princeton University Press, Princeton, New Jersey, 1979.

What is: "What is this place" by Huub Oosterhuis, translated by David Smith. Copyright © 1967, Gooi en Sticht, bv., Baarn, The Netherlands. Published by OCP Publications, Portland, Oregon. All rights reserved. Used with permission.

Is there then: From *The Church Incarnate* by Rudolf Schwarz, Copyright © 1958, Henry Regnery Company. All rights reserved. Reprinted by special permission of Regnery Publishing, Inc., Washington, D. C.

One of the: From *The Book of Tea* by Okakura Kakuzo. Published by Charles E. Tuttle Company, Rutland, Vermont.

The house is: From "Building Blocks" by Aidan Kavanagh in Summer: *GIA Quarterly*, vol. 4, no. 4. Published by GIA Publications, Inc., Chicago.

It is clear: From *The Early Churches of Constantinople: Architecture and Liturgy* by Thomas F. Mathews. Copyright © 1971, The Pennsylvania State University. Reprinted by permission of The Pennsylvania State University Press, University Park and London.

Here is born: From *The Shape of Baptism: The Rite of Christian Initiation* by Aidan Kavanagh. Copyright © 1978, Pueblo Publishing Co., Inc. Reprinted by permission of The Liturgical Press, Collegeville, Minnesota.

We shape: From *The Ministry of Liturgical Movement* by Thomas G. Simons and James M. Fitzpatrick. Published by The Liturgical Press, 1984.

If you let: From *A Primal Spirit: Ten Contemporary Japanese Sculptors* by Howard N. Fox. Published by the Los Angeles County Museum of Art, 1990.

(50) **Worship within:** From *The Urban Character of Christian Worship* by John F. Baldovin, SJ. Published by Pont. Institutium Studiorum Orientalium, Rome, 1987.

To search the: From *The Isamu Noguchi Garden Museum* by Isamu Noguchi. Copyright © 1987, Isamu Noguchi. Published by Harry N. Abrams, Inc. Used with permission.

Speaking of hearing: From *The Arts Without Mystery* by Denis Donoghue. Published by Little, Brown and Company, Boston, 1983.

Admittedly: From *Public Worship: A Survey* by Josef A. Jungmann, SJ. Copyright © 1957, The Order of St. Benedict. Reprinted with permission of The Liturgical Press, Collegeville, Minnesota.

The artist: From *The Environment for Worship: A Reader,* 1980. Reprinted by permission of the United States Catholic Conference, Washington, D. C.

The charge against: From *Christian Century,* p. 925.

Faith grows: From *Music in Catholic Worship.* Reprinted by permission of the United States Catholic Conference, Washington, D. C.

For art in itself: From *Art, Creativity and the Sacred* edited by Diane Apostolos-Cappadona. Reprinted with permission of The Crossroad Publishing Company, New York.

Long long with wonder: "Ecce Homo" From *Delusions, Etc.* Copyright © 1969, 1971, John Berryman. Reprinted by permission of Farrar, Straus and Giroux Inc.

The singers who sing: From *Ministry through Word and Sacrament* by Thomas C. Oden. Published by The Crossroad Publishing Company, New York, 1989. Reprinted by permission of the author.

At the most: From *Art, Creativity and the Sacred* edited by Diane Apostolos-Cappadona. Reprinted with permission of The Crossroad Publishing Company, New York.

So the sermon: From *Telling the Truth* by Frederick Buechner. Copyright © 1977, Frederick Buechner. Reprinted by permission of HarperCollins Publishers, Inc.

I know that: From *Dancing at the Edge of the World* by Ursula K. Le Guin. English translation copyright © 1972, Ben Belitt. Used by permission of Grove/Atlantic, Inc., New York.

All-seeing Father: From *Saint Gregory Nazianzen: Selected Poems* translated by John McGuckin. Copyright © 1986, The Sisters of the Love of God. Reprinted with permission of SLG Press, Oxford, England.

It is not: From *Invisible Cities.* Published by Harcourt Brace Jovanovich, New York, 1974.

The homily: Reprinted from *Worshipful Preaching* by Gerard Sloyan. Copyright © 1984, Fortress Press. Used with permission of Augsburg Fortress.

Be careful: "Amen" in *Assembly,* February 1981. Reprinted with permission of Notre Dame Center for Pastoral Liturgy.

Those who run: Reprinted with permission of Scribner's, an imprint of Simon & Schuster from *Man's Quest for God* by Abraham Joshua Heschel. Copyright © 1954, Abraham Joshua Heschel; copyright renewed © 1982, Hannah Susannah Heschel and Sylvia Heschel.

Indeed there: Reprinted with permission of Scribner's, an imprint of Simon & Schuster from *Man's Quest for God* by Abraham Joshua Heschel.

(60) **Words strain:** Excerpt from "Burnt Norton" in *Four Quartets.* Copyright © 1943, T.S. Eliot; renewed 1971, Esme Valerie Eliot. Reprinted by permission of Harcourt Brace and Company.

We cannot apprehend: From *A Primal Spirit: Ten Contemporary Japanese Sculptors* by Howard N. Fox. Published by the Los Angeles County Museum of Art, 1990.

Everything must have: "A Christening" by Robert Kelly. Copyright © 1981, Robert Kelly. Reprinted from *Spiritual Exercises* with permission of Black Sparrow Press.

We put thirty: From *Notan: The Dark-Light Principle of Design* by Dorr Bothwell and Marlys Mayfield. Copyright © 1968, Litton Educational Publishing, Inc. Reprinted with permission of Dover Publications, Inc., New York.

Silence is: "Silence" in *Assembly,* September 1982. Reprinted with permission of Notre Dame Center for Pastoral Liturgy.

What does the word: From *Davita's Harp* by Chaim Potok. Published by Fawcett Crest Books, New York, 1986.

Follow, poet: From *Collected Poems* by W. H. Auden. Copyright © 1940 and renewed 1968, W. H. Auden. Reprinted by permission of Random House, Inc., New York.

Prayer the Churches: From *The English Poems of George Herbert* edited by C. A. Patrides. Published by Rowman and Littlefield, Lanham, Maryland, 1977.

My God: From *Devotions Upon Emergent Occasions* by John Donne. Published by The University of Michigan Press, Ann Arbor, 1960.

The auditory: From *The Arts Without Mystery* by Denis Donoghue. Published by Little, Brown and Company, Boston, 1983.

Lengthy explanations: From *Elements of Rite: A Handbook of Liturgical Style* by Aidan Kavanagh. Copyright © 1982, Pueblo Publishing Co., Inc. Reprinted by permission of The Liturgical Press, Collegeville, Minnesota.

Ritual, symbol: From *Worship* by Evelyn Underhill. Copyright © 1936, Harper & Row Publishers, Inc. Copyright renewed. Reprinted by permission of HarperCollins Publishers, Inc.

God hates: From *Parochial and Plain Sermons* by John Henry Newman. Published by Ignatius Press, San Francisco.

The Spirit begins: From *The Wellspring of Worship* by Jean Corbon, translated by Matthew J. O'Connell. English translation copyright © 1988, The Missionary Society of St. Paul the Apostle. Reprinted by permission of Paulist Press, New York.

Some years ago: From "Christian Formation of Children: The Role of Ritual and Celebration" in *Liturgy and Spirituality in Context: Perspectives on Prayer and Culture* edited by Eleanor Bernstein, CSJ. Reprinted with permission of The Liturgical Press.

The liturgy: From *The Early Churches of Constantinople: Architecture and Liturgy* by Thomas F. Mathews. Copyright © 1971, The Pennsylvania State University. Reprinted by permission of The Pennsylvania State University Press, University Park and London.

Next the priest: From *The Fathers of the Church: The Works of Saint Cyril of Jerusalem,* translated by Leo P. McCauley, SJ, and Anthony A. Stephenson. Published by the Catholic University of America Press, Washington, D. C.

What is procession: "Processing" in *Assembly,* December 1979. Reprinted with permission of Notre Dame Center for Pastoral Liturgy.

Those whose task: "Liturgical Crisis" in *Assembly,* April 1986. Reprinted with permission of Notre Dame Center for Pastoral Liturgy. (70)

Then the Deacon: From *St. Cyril of Jerusalem's Lectures on the Christian Sacraments* edited by F. L. Cross. Reprinted by permission of St. Vladimir's Seminary Press, Crestwood, New York.

When the good: From *Sacred Signs* by Romano Guardini, translated by Grace Branham. Published by Pio Decimo Press, St. Louis, Missouri, 1956.

The principal thing: From *The Art of Prayer: An Orthodox Anthology* compiled by Igumen Chariton of Valamo, translated by E. Kadloubovsky and E. M. Palmer. Reprinted by permission of Faber and Faber, Ltd.

More is: From *Art, Creativity and the Sacred* edited by Diane Apostolos-Cappadona. Reprinted with permission of The Crossroad Publishing Company, New York.

After situating: From *Beloved* by Toni Morrison. Copyright © 1987, Toni Morrison. Reprinted by permission of International Creative Management, Inc.

When we cross: From *How Firm a Foundation: Voices of the Early Liturgical Movement* compiled by Kathleen Hughes, RSCJ. Published by Liturgy Training Publications, Chicago, 1990.

Christians often ask: From *Man and His Symbols.* Published by Doubleday Publishing Company, 1969.

Zedekiah: "Bowing" in *Assembly,* December 1979. Reprinted with permission of Notre Dame Center for Pastoral Liturgy.

There is no: From *Confucius: The Secular as Sacred* by Herbert Fingarette. Copyright © 1972, Herbert Fingarette. Reprinted by permission of Harper-Collins Publishers, Inc.

Rites symbolize: From *The Other Dimension.* Published by Seabury Press, New York, 1979.

The liturgy: From *On Liturgical Theology* by Aidan Kavanagh. Copyright © 1984, Pueblo Publishing Co., Inc. Reprinted by permission of The Liturgical Press, Collegeville, Minnesota.

Anamnesis: From *Contemplative Participation* by Mary Collins, OSB, Copyright © 1990, The Order of St. Benedict. Reprinted with permission of The Liturgical Press, Collegeville, Minnesota.

The island: From *Teaching a Stone to Talk* by Annie Dillard. Copyright © 1982, Annie Dillard. Reprinted by permission of HarperCollins Publishers, Inc.

(50) **The assembly:** From "Assembly: Remembering the People of God" in *Pastoral Music,* August-September 1983.

Take care: From *The Catholic Study Bible.* Published by Oxford University Press, New York, 1990.

Step by step: From *Dakota.* Copyright © 1993, KathleenNorris. Reprinted by permission of Ticknor & Fields/Houghton Mifflin Co. All rights reserved.

Spirit: From *Liturgy and Architecture* by Louis Bouyer. Copyright © 1973, University of Notre Dame Press. Used with permission.

Those of us: From *Worship: Reforming Tradition* by Thomas J. Talley. Copyright © 1990, The Pastoral Press, Washington, D. C. Used with permission.

When the patient: From *The Screwtape Letters* by C. S. Lewis. Copyright © 1942, C. S. Lewis. Used with permission of HarperCollins Publishers, Ltd.

Father, why does: From *Father McGuire's New Baltimore Catechism and Mass.* Reprinted by permission of Benziger Publishing Company.

Obedience is: From *Spiritual Life: A Quarterly of Contemporary Spirituality,* Summer 1991. Published by the Washington Province of the Discalced Carmelite Friars, Inc., Washington, D. C.

Any theory: From *The Magic of Ritual.* Published by HarperSanFrancisco, 1992.

The Justice of God: From *Liturgy and Social Justice* edited by Mark Searle. Copyright © 1980, The Order of St. Benedict. Reprinted with permission of The Liturgical Press.

The world is: From *The Norton Anthology of Poetry.* Published by W. W. Norton & Company, Inc., New York.

In the biblical: From *For the Life of the World: Sacraments and Orthodoxy* by Alexander Schmemann. Copyright © 1963, 1970, 1971, 1973, Alexander Schmemann. Reprinted by permission of St. Vladimir's Seminary Press, Crestwood, New York.

The fruitful: From *Bread in the Wilderness* by Thomas Merton. Copyright © 1953, Our Lady of Gethsemani Monastery. Reprinted with permission of The Liturgical Press.

We can interrupt: From *For the Life of the World: Sacraments and Orthodoxy* by Alexander Schmemann. Copyright © 1963, 1970, 1971, 1973, Alexander Schmemann. Reprinted by permission of St. Vladimir's Seminary Press, Crestwood, New York.

Before we can: From *The Eucharist and the Hunger of the World* by Monika K. Hellwig. Copyright © 1976, The Missionary Society of St. Paul the Apostle. Reprinted by permission of Paulist Press, New York.

And I shall: From *The Prayers of Catherine of Siena* edited by Suzanne Noffke, OP. Copyright © 1983, Suzanne Noffke, OP. Reprinted by permission of Paulist Press, New York.

Near the end: From "Scholars Say Liturgy Still a Mystery" in *National Catholic Reporter,* 1985.

Elected Silence: From *The Norton Anthology of Poetry.* Published by W. W. Norton & Company, Inc., New York.

Rejoicing the church: From *The Fathers of the Church: Saint Ambrose,* translated by Roy J. Deferrari. Published by the Catholic University of America Press, Washington, D. C., 1963.

You are drunk: "But Not With Wine" by Jessica (90) Powers. Reprinted from *The House at Rest* with permission of the Carmelite Monastery, Pewaukee, Wisconsin.

If, then, you wish: From *Message of the Fathers of the Church: The Eucharist* by Daniel J. Sheerin. Published by Michael Glazier, Inc., Wilmington, Delaware, 1986.

Certainty of the elect: "Early Christian Eucharist" by Robert Kelly. Copyright © 1981, Robert Kelly. Reprinted from *Spiritual Exercises* with permission of Black Sparrow Press.

What is most: From "The Preparatory Rites: A Case Study in Liturgical Ecology" in *Worship,* January 1993. Reprinted by permission of St. John's Abbey, Collegeville, Minnesota.

We are the body: From *Communion in Australian Churches,* Joint Board of Christian Education in Melbourne.

When I nourish: From *Human Meal to Christian Eucharist* by Philippe Rouillard. Published by The Liturgical Press, Collegeville, Minnesota.

As practiced: From *Unsearchable Riches: The Symbolic Nature of Liturgy* by David N. Power, OMI. Reprinted by permission of The Liturgical Press, Collegeville, Minnesota.

We have just: From the last speech of Archbishop Romero on March 24, 1980.

At the heart: From The *Shape of the Liturgy* by Dom Gregory Dix. Published by Dacre Press, Adam and Charles Black, London. Used with permission.

Now about: Reprinted from *Early Christian Fathers* edited by Cyril C. Richardson. Volume I: *The Library of Christian Classics.* Used by permission of Westminster John Knox Press.

Those who have: Reprinted from *Early Christian Fathers* edited by Cyril C. Richardson. Volume I: *The Library of Christian Classics.* Used by permission of Westminster John Knox Press.

After the people: From *The Mass of the Roman Rite* by Joseph A. Jungmann, SJ. Reprinted by permission of Benziger Publishing Company.

(100) **I used to look:** From *Christianity Rediscovered.* Published by Orbis Books, Maryknoll, New York.

Our surrender: From "On Ritually Remembering Zion by the Streams of Babylon" in *Living Worship,* vol. 11, no. 6. Copyright The Liturgical Conference, 8750 Georgia Avenue, Suite 123, Silver Spring MD 20910-3621. All rights reserved. Used with permission.

A word: From *Worship and Secular Man* by Raimundo Panikkar. Published by Orbis Books, Maryknoll, New York, 1973.

Exploitation: From *The Sacred Play of Children* by Diane Apostolos-Cappadona. Copyright © 1983, Center for Pastoral Liturgy of the Catholic University of America. Reprinted by permission of Harper-Collins Publishers, Inc.

Persons of intelligence: From *Faith, Culture and the Worshiping Community* by Michael Warren. Published by The Pastoral Press, Washington, D. C., 1993.

The Christian liturgy: From *The Sacred Play of Children* by Diane Apostolos-Cappadona. Copyright © 1983, Center for Pastoral Liturgy of the Catholic University of America. Reprinted by permission of HaperCollins Publishers, Inc.

Our problem: Reprinted with permission of Scribner's, an imprint of Simon & Schuster from *Man's Quest for God* by Abraham Joshua Heschel. Copyright © 1954, Abraham Joshua Heschel; copyright renewed © 1982, Hannah Susannah Heschel and Sylvia Heschel.

But anyway: Excerpt from *The Habit of Being,* edited by Sally Fitzgerald. Copyright © 1979, Regina O'Connor. Reprinted by permission of Farrar, Straus and Giroux, Inc.

When the guru: From *The Song of the Bird* by Anthony deMello. Copyright © 1982, Anthony deMello. Used by permission of Doubleday, a division of Bantam Doubleday Dell Publishing Group, Inc.

Addressing God: From *The Changing Face of Jewish and Christian Worship in North America* edited by P. Bradshaw and L. Hoffman. Copyright © 1991, University of Notre Dame Press. Used with permission.

Those who plead: Reprinted with permission of Scribner's, an imprint of Simon & Schuster from *Man's Quest for God* by Abraham Joshua Heschel. Copyright © 1954, Abraham Joshua Heschel; copyright renewed © 1982, Hannah Susannah Heschel and Sylvia Heschel.

After many years: From *After Christendom?* Published by Abingdon Press, 1991.

Full, active: From *Liturgical Ministry,* Spring 1992.

For Christians: From *Life Together* by Dietrich Bonhoeffer. English translation copyright © 1954, Harper & Brothers; copyright renewed 1982, Helen S. Doberstein. Reprinted by permission of Harper-Collins Publishers, Inc.

The cloud of cells: From "The Origin of the Praise of God" in *This Body Is Made of Camphor and Gopherwood* by Robert Bly. Published by Harper and Row Publishers, 1977.

Each day: From *Introduction to Liturgical* Theology by Alexander Schmemann, translated by Asheleigh E. Moorhouse. Translation copyright © 1966, Asheleigh Moorhouse. Reprinted by permission of St. Vladimir's Seminary Press, Crestwood, New York.

We bring: "I Confess" in *Assembly,* February 1983. Reprinted with permission of Notre Dame Center for Pastoral Liturgy.

O Radiant Light: From *Worship,* #12. Text copyright © Wiilam Storey.

O splendor: From *The Presbyterian Hymnal,* #474.

10) **One of the:** From *Dakota.* Copyright © 1993, KathleenNorris. Reprinted by permission of Ticknor & Fields/Houghton Mifflin Co. All rights reserved.

The Visitor shuffled: Except from *The Spire.* Copyright © 1964; renewed 1992, William Golding. Reprinted by permission of Harcourt Brace and Company.

Christ, mighty Savior: From *Hymnal for the Hours.* Published by GIA Publications, Inc., Chicago, 1989.

We read and reread: From *Working the Angles: The Shape of Pastoral Integrity* by Eugene H. Peterson. Published by Wm. B. Eerdmans Publishing Co., 1987. Used with permission.

Prayer: From *The Norton Anthology of Poetry.* Published by W. W. Norton & Company, Inc., New York.

Strive to render: From *Early Fathers from the Philokalia* translated by G. E. H. Palmer and E. Kadleigh. Reprinted by permission of Faber and Faber, Ltd.

Before all else: From *Ministry through Word and Sacrament* by Thomas C. Oden. Published by The Crossroad Publishing Company, New York, 1989. Reprinted by permission of the author.

After the maggid's: From *Tales of the Hasidim: The Early Masters* by Martin Buber. Published by Schocken Books, New York, 1978.

You have first: From *As Bread That Is Broken* by Peter G. van Breemen, SJ. Published by Dimension Books, Inc. Denville, New Jersey, 1974.

Applaud: From *Lyric Psalms: Half a Psalter* by Francis Patrick Sullivan. Copyright © 1983, National Association of Pastoral Musicians, Washington, D. C. Used with permission.

Why is the: From *The Sunday Sermons of the Great Fathers,* vol. 2, by M. F. Toal. Copyright © 1958, Henry Regnery Company. All rights reserved. Reprinted by special permission of Regnery Publishing, Inc., Washington, D. C.

To do justice: From *The Eternal Year* by Karl Rahner, SJ. Published by Helicon Press, Baltimore, Maryland.

On this day: From *The Catholic Study Bible.* Published by Oxford University Press, New York, 1990.

This is the day: From *For the Life of the World: Sacraments and Orthodoxy* by Alexander Schmemann. Copyright © 1963, 1970, 1971, 1973, Alexander Schmemann. Reprinted by permission of St. Vladimir's Seminary Press, Crestwood, New York.

On every: Reprinted from *Early Christian Fathers* edited by Cyril C. Richardson. Volume I: *The Library of Christian Classics.* Used by permission of Westminster John Knox Press.

By a tradition: Excerpt from the English translation of *Documents on the Liturgy, 1963–1979: Conciliar, Papal and Curial Texts.* Copyright © 1982, International Committee on English in the Liturgy, Inc. All rights reserved.

In the course: "Keeping Sunday" in *Assembly,* June (120) 1981. Reprinted with permission of Notre Dame Center for Pastoral Liturgy.

Since it is Sunday: From *Egeria: Diary of a Pilgrimage* translated by George E. Gingras. Published by Newman Press, New York, 1970.

When all work: Excerpts from *The Sabbath.* Copyright © 1951, Abraham Joshua Heschel; renewed 1979, Sylvia Heschel. Reprinted by permission of Farrar, Straus and Giroux, Inc.

What exactly: From *Pastoral Liturgy* by J. A. Jungmann, SJ. Published by Herder and Herder, New York, 1962.

Christ has said: From *The Eternal Year* by Karl Rahner, SJ. Published by Helicon Press, Baltimore, Maryland.

Someone may: From *In Tune with the World: A Theory of Festivity* by Joseph Pieper and Clara Winston. Published by Harcourt Brace & World, Inc., Orlando, Florida, 1965. Original in German: Zustimmung zur Welt (Kosel, Munchen 1964). Used with permission of Kosel-Verlag GmbH & Co., Munich, Germany.

Liturgy then: From *The Church's Year of Grace* by Dr. Pius Parsch. Copyright © 1957, The Order of St. Benedict. Reprinted with permission of The Liturgical Press.

Let the Catholic: From *The Liturgical Year* by Abbot Gueranger, OSB. Published by The Newman Press, New York, 1948.

It is true: Excerpt form *Seasons of Celebration.* Copyright © 1965, Abbey of Gethsemani; renewed 1993, Trustees of the Merton Legacy Trust. Reprinted by permission of Farrar, Straus and Giroux, Inc.

It may well: From *Art, Creativity and the Sacred* edited by Diane Apostolos-Cappadona. Reprinted with permission of The Crossroad Publishing Company, New York.

We are always: From *For the Life of the World: Sacraments and Orthodoxy* by Alexander Schmemann. Copyright © 1963, 1970, 1971, 1973, Alexander Schmemann. Reprinted by permission of St. Vladimir's Seminary Press, Crestwood, New York.

I am speaking: From "The Eucharist as a 'Hungry Feast' and the Appropriateness of Our Want" in *Living Worship*, vol. 13, no. 9. Copyright The Liturgical Conference, 8750 Georgia Avenue, Suite 123, Silver Spring MD 20910-3621. All rights reserved. Used with permission.

Likewise: From *Theology of Hope* by Jurgen Moltmann, translated by James W. Leitsch. Published by Harper & Row Publishers, New York, 1967.

Of course: From *The All of It* by Jeannette Haien. Published by Harper & Row Publishers, New York, 1986.

All art: From *The Picture of Dorian Gray* by Oscar Wilde. Published by Penguin Books, 1975.

As I go: From *Changing Women, Changing Church* edited by Marie Louise Uhr. Published by Millennium Books, Newtown NSW Australia, 1992. Used with permission.

Spits of glitter: Reprinted from *Collected Poems 1951–1971* by A. R. Ammons, with the permission of W. W. Norton & Company, Inc. Copyright © 1972, A. R. Ammons.

(130) **In the Christian ritual:** From "The Mysteries" in the *Bollingen Series.* Copyright © 1955, Bollingen Foundation, Inc., New York. Published by Princeton University Press, Princeton, New Jersey.

Commentators have: Reprinted with permission of Scribner's, an imprint of Simon & Schuster from *Man's Quest for God* by Abraham Joshua Heschel. Copyright © 1954, Abraham Joshua Heschel; copyright renewed © 1982, Hannah Susannah Heschel and Sylvia Heschel.

Ritual is not: From *The Feast of Fools: A Theological Essay on Festivity and Fantasy* by Harvey Cox. Published by Harvard University Press, Cambridge, Massachusetts.

The eighteenth-century: From *Teaching a Stone to Talk* by Annie Dillard. Copyright © 1982, Annie Dillard. Reprinted by permission of HarperCollins Publishers, Inc.

Man, my friends: From *Babette's Feast and Other Anecdotes of Destiny* by Isak Dinesen. Copyright © 1953, 1958; renewed 1981, 1986, Isak Dinesen. Reprinted by permission of Random House, Inc.

When was the last: From "Ideas and Illustrations" by David K. McMillan in *Homily Service,* October 1993.

I return: From "A Woman Gives a Feast: Transforming Rituals in Old Age" in *Liturgy: And at the Last.* Copyright The Liturgical Conference, 8750 Georgia Avenue, Suite 123, Silver Spring MD 20910-3621. All rights reserved. Used with permission.

We enter a house: "The Fragrance of Feasting" in *Assembly,* May 1993. Reprinted with permission of Notre Dame Center for Pastoral Liturgy.

I've known rivers: From *The Norton Anthology of Poetry.* Published by W. W. Norton & Company, Inc., New York.

Never say: From *Hymn of the Universe* by Pierre Teilhard de Chardin. Copyright © 1961, Editions du Seuil; English translation © 1965, William Collins Sons & Co., Ltd., and Harper & Row. Copyright renewed. Reprinted by permission of HarperCollins Publishers, Inc.

Earth's command: From *Familiar Quotations* by John Bartlett. Published by Little, Brown and Company, Boston, 1968.

Christianity is not: From *For the Life of the World: Sacraments and Orthodoxy* by Alexander Schmemann. Copyright © 1963, 1970, 1971, 1973, Alexander Schmemann. Reprinted by permission of St. Vladimir's Seminary Press, Crestwood, New York.

It is plain: From *Worship* by Evelyn Underhill. Copyright © 1936, Harper & Row Publishers, Inc. Copyright renewed. Reprinted by permission of HarperCollins Publishers, Inc.

The man Jesus: From *Christ the Sacrament of the Encounter with God* by E. Schillebeeckx, OP. Reprinted by permission of Sheed & Ward, Inc., New York.

Sacraments do not: From *Christ Acts Through the Sacraments* by A.-M Roguet, OP. Reprinted with permission of The Liturgical Press, Collegeville, Minnesota.

Christians have not: From *Environment and Art in Catholic Worship,* 1978. Reprinted by permission of the United States Catholic Conference, Washington, D. C.

All of this: From *The Heythrop Journal: A Quarterly Review of Philosophy and Theology,* July 1978. Published by Heythrop College, University of London.

Despite common: From "Symbols Are Actions, Not Objects" in *Living Worship,* vol. 13, no. 2. Copyright The Liturgical Conference, 8750 Georgia

Avenue, Suite 123, Silver Spring MD 20910-3621. All rights reserved. Used with permission.

There is nothing: From *The Feast of Fools: A Theological Essay on Festivity and Fantasy* by Harvey Cox. Published by Harvard University Press, Cambridge, Massachusetts.

When we enter: From *Worship* by Evelyn Underhill. Copyright © 1936, Harper & Row Publishers, Inc. Copyright renewed. Reprinted by permission of HarperCollins Publishers, Inc.

You were led: From *Readings for the Daily Office from the Early Church* by J. Robert Wright. Published by The Church Hymnal Corporation, New York, 1991. Reprinted by permission of General Theological Seminary, New York.

Every word: From *Environment and Art in Catholic Worship*, 1978. Reprinted by permission of the United States Catholic Conference, Washington, D. C.

Is that everything: From *The Heart of the Matter* by Graham Greene. Published by Penguin Books in association with William Heinemann, Ltd., 1978.

One who is: From *Elements of Rite: A Handbook of Liturgical Style* by Aidan Kavanagh. Copyright © 1982, Pueblo Publishing Co., Inc. Reprinted by permission of The Liturgical Press, Collegeville, Minnesota.

It is precisely: From *Blessed and Broken: An Exploration of the Contemporary Experience of God in Eucharistic Celebration* by Ralph A. Keifer. Published by Michael Glazier, Inc., Wilmington, Delaware, 1982.

A myth: From *Dynamics of Faith* by Paul Tillich. Published by Harper & Brothers, New York, 1957.

Assembling: From "Now the Sacred Words are Done: Liturgy in a Post-Translation Era" in *Living Worship*, vol. 12, no. 5. Copyright The Liturgical Conference, 8750 Georgia Avenue, Suite 123, Silver Spring MD 20910-3621. All rights reserved. Used with permission.

I don't pray: From *Jacob the Baker* by Noah benShea. Published by Villard Books, New York, 1989.

Christian liturgy: From "What Does Liturgy Do?" in *Worship*, May 1992. Reprinted by permission of St. John's Abbey, Collegeville, Minnesota.

Many people: From *The Way of a Pilgrim* by R. M. French. Copyright © 1965, Mrs. Eleanor French. Copyright renewed. Reprinted by permission of HarperCollins Publishers, Inc.

The Lord could: From *Parable of Community* by Brother Roger of Taizé. Published by A. R. Mowbray & Co., Ltd., Oxford, England, 1984.

The liturgy: Reprinted with the permission of Macmillan Publishing Company from *The American Parish and the Roman Liturgy* by H. A. Reinhold. Copyright © 1958, H. A. Reinhold.

The rugged: From "The Amen Corner" in *Worship*, March 1992. Reprinted by permission of St. John's Abbey, Collegeville, Minnesota.

What matters: From *Worship*, published by The Westminster Press, 1982.

Remember Lord: From *Byzantine Daily Worship*. Reprinted with permission of Alleluia Press, Allendale, New Jersey.

Why the Lord: Excerpt from the English translation of *The Liturgy of the Hours*. Copyright © 1974, International Committee on English in the Liturgy, Inc. All rights reserved.

O deep unknown: From *Candles in Babylon* by (150) Denise Levertov. Copyright © 1982, Denise Levertov. Reprinted by pemission of New Directions Publishing Corporation, New York.

Open the eyes: From *Ministry through Word and Sacrament* by Thomas C. Oden. Published by The Crossroad Publishing Company, New York, 1989. Reprinted by permission of the author.

Dawdling: From *Anthology of Australian Religious Poetry*. Published by Collins Dove Publishers, a division of HarperCollins Publishers, 1986.

Evening prayer: From *Life Together* by Dietrich Bonhoeffer. English translation copyright © 1954, Harper & Brothers; copyright renewed 1982, Helen S. Doberstein. Reprinted by permission of Harper-Collins Publishers, Inc.

To me: From *Dakota*. Copyright © 1993, Kathleen Norris. Reprinted by permission of Ticknor & Fields/ Houghton Mifflin Co. All rights reserved.

Is neighborhood: From *Contemplative Participation* by Mary Collins, OSB. Copyright © 1990, The Order of St. Benedict. Reprinted with permission of The Liturgical Press, Collegeville, Minnesota.

Of all the institutions: From *Hunger of Memory* by Richard Rodriguez. Published by David R. Godine Publisher, Inc., Boston, 1982.

Even allowing: From *Worship: Reforming Tradition* by Thomas J. Talley. Copyright © 1990, The Pastoral Press, Washington, D. C. Used with permission.

I was obviously: From *Bluebeard*, Published by Delacorte Press, 1987.

And Sunday: From *Liturgy: Covenant with the World.* Copyright The Liturgical Conference, 8750 Georgia Avenue, Suite 123, Silver Spring MD 20910-3621. All rights reserved. Used with permission.

Ministers must not: From *Elements of Rite: A Handbook of Liturgical Style* by Aidan Kavanagh. Copyright © 1982, Pueblo Publishing Co., Inc. Reprinted by permission of The Liturgical Press, Collegeville, Minnesota.

When you are: From *Joy of Cooking* by Irma S. Rombauer and Mrion Rombauer Becker. Published by The Bobbs-Merrill Company, Inc., Indianapolis/New York.

Seriousness: From *Dry Bones: Living Worship Guides to Good Liturgy.* Copyright The Liturgical Conference, 8750 Georgia Avenue, Suite 123, Silver Spring MD 20910-3621. All rights reserved. Used with permission.

Saint Benedict: From *Contemplative Participation* by Mary Collins, OSB, Copyright © 1990, The Order of St. Benedict. Reprinted with permission of The Liturgical Press.

Communities: From *With a Daughter's Eye* by Mary Catherine Bateson. Published by Pocket Books, New York, 1985.

Ritual is a system: From *Elements of Rite: A Handbook of Liturgical Style* by Aidan Kavanagh. Copyright © 1982, Pueblo Publishing Co., Inc. Reprinted by permission of The Liturgical Press, Collegeville, Minnesota.

She began with: Excerpt from "The Sojourner," *The Ballad of the Sad Cafe and Collected Short Stories.* Copyright 1963, 1941, 1942, 1950; © 1955, Carson McCullers; © renewed 1979, Floria V. Lasky. Reprinted by permission of Houghton Mifflin Company. All rights reserved.

Regularity is beautiful: From *Shaker Furniture: The Craftsmanship of an American Communal Sect* by Edward Deming Andrews and Faith Andrews. Copyright © 1937, 1964, Edward Deming Andrews and Faith Andrews. Reprinted with permission of Dover Publications, Inc., New York.

Have nothing: From *Shaker Furniture: The Craftsmanship of an American Communal Sect* by Edward Deming Andrews and Faith Andrews. Copyright © 1937, 1964, Edward Deming Andrews and Faith Andrews. Reprinted with permission of Dover Publications, Inc., New York.

A religious ritual: From *Worship* by Evelyn Underhill. Copyright © 1936, Harper & Row Publishers, Inc. Copyright renewed. Reprinted by permission of HarperCollins Publishers, Inc.

These forms are: Reprinted from *Three Books about (1* the Church by William Loehe, translated by James L. Schauf. Copyright © 1969, Fortress Press. Used with permission of Augsburg Fortress.

A high school stage: From *Teaching a Stone to Talk* by Annie Dillard. Copyright © 1982, Annie Dillard. Reprinted by permission of HarperCollins Publishers, Inc.

Liturgical celebration: From *Dry Bones: Living Worship Guides to Good Liturgy.* Copyright The Liturgical Conference, 8750 Georgia Avenue, Suite 123, Silver Spring MD 20910-3621. All rights reserved. Used with permission.

In liturgy: From "The Amen Corner" in *Worship,* September 1992. Reprinted by permission of St. John's Abbey, Collegeville, Minnesota.

Popular religiosity: From *Popular Catholicism: A Hispanic Perspective* by Arturo Perez.

The clichés: From *Multi-Media Worship: A Model and Nine Viewpoints* edited by Myron B. Bloy, Jr. Published by The Seabury Press, New York, 1969.

It's only modern: From *The Arts Without Mystery* by Denis Donoghue. Published by Little, Brown and Company, Boston, 1983.

God may be: Reprinted with permission of Scribner's, an imprint of Simon & Schuster from *Man's Quest for God* by Abraham Joshua Heschel. Copyright © 1954, Abraham Joshua Heschel; copyright renewed © 1982, Hannah Susannah Heschel and Sylvia Heschel.

The world: From *Theological Investigations,* vol. xiv, translated by David Bourke. Reprinted by permission of The Crossroad Publishing Company.

As the most basic: From *The Liturgy of the World: Karl Rahner's Theology of Worship* by Michael Skelley, SJ. Copyright © 1991, The Order of St. Benedict, Inc. Reprinted by permission of The Liturgical Press, Collegeville, Minnesota.

To landscape: From "The Amen Corner" in *Worship,* March 1992. Reprinted by permission of St. John's Abbey, Collegeville, Minnesota.

If then, praise: From *God the Future of Man* by E. Schillebeeckx, OP. Reprinted by permission of Sheed & Ward, Inc., New York.

Reconciliation: From *Background and Directions,* vol. 3 in *The Rite of Penance: Commentaries.* Copyright The Liturgical Conference, 8750 Georgia Avenue, Suite 123, Silver Spring MD 20910-3621. All rights reserved. Used with permission.

When you have: From *Luther's Works,* vol. 35 in *Word and Sacrament,* edited by E. Theodore

Bachmann. Published by Concordia Publishing House and Muhlenberg Press, Philadelphia, 1960.

For centuries: From *Pastoral Liturgy* by J. A. Jungmann, SJ. Published by Herder and Herder, New York, 1962.

The doom-sayers: "Reform of Symbols: The Present Task" in *Assembly,* June 1983. Reprinted with permission of Notre Dame Center for Pastoral Liturgy.

Liturgy rather: From *Worship: Renewal to Practice* by Mary Collins, OSB. Copyright © 1987, The Pastoral Press, Washington, D. C. Used with permission.

For to my: From *English Catholic Worship* edited by J. D. Crichton, H. E. Winstone and J. R. Ainslie. Published by Cassell Ltd., London, 1979.

70) **The Sacred Council:** Excerpt from the English translation of *Documents on the Liturgy, 1963–1979:* Conciliar, Papal and Curial Texts. Copyright © 1982, International Committee on English in the Liturgy, Inc. All rights reserved.

From the Greek: From *Theological Dictionary* edited by Cornelius Ernst, OP, translated by Richard Strachan. Published by Herder and Herder, New York, 1968.

Unfortunately: Excerpt from *Letters from Vatican City.* Copyright © 1963, Farrar, Straus and Company; renewed 1991, Farrar, Straus and Giroux, Inc. Used with permission.

A new inspiration: From *Fiesta, Worship and Family* by Ricardo Ramirez, CSB. Distributed by MACC Distribution Center, San Antonio, Texas.

Liturgical prayer: From *The Liturgical Year* by Abbot Gueranger, OSB. Published by The Newman Press, New York, 1948.

Now it would be: Excerpt from *Seasons of Celebration.* Copyright © 1965, Abbey of Gethsemani; renewed 1993, Trustees of the Merton Legacy Trust. Reprinted by permission of Farrar, Straus and Giroux, Inc.

Many of us: From *Liturgy and Life, a Pastoral Letter* by Richard Cardinal Cushing. Reprinted with permission of the Archdiocese of Boston.

The revisions: From *Sacramental Liturgy* by Frederick R. McManus. Published by Herder and Herder, New York, 1967.

Everywhere I go: From *The Mass in Time of Doubt* by Ralph A. Keifer. Copyright © 1983, National Association of Pastoral Musicians, Washington, D. C. Used with permission.

The Sunday liturgy: From *Elements of Rite: A Handbook of Liturgical Style* by Aidan Kavanagh.

Copyright © 1982, Pueblo Publishing Co., Inc. Reprinted by permission of The Liturgical Press, Collegeville, Minnesota.

Unless Christian: From *Worship: Renewal to Practice* by Mary Collins, OSB. Copyright © 1987, The Pastoral Press, Washington, D. C. Used with permission.

The greatest gift: From *Praying Our Experiences* by Joseph F. Schmidt, FSC. Published by Saint Mary's Press, Christian Brothers Publications, Winona, Minnesota, 1980.

Each church: From *Environment and Art in Catholic Worship,* 1978. Reprinted by permission of the United States Catholic Conference, Washington, D.C.